Heroic
ADVENTURES
Anthology

SERIES EDITORS
Margaret Iveson
Samuel Robinson

EDITORIAL CONSULTANT
Alan Simpson

LITERATURE CONSULTANT
Rivka Cranley

TEACHER CONSULTANTS
Dirk Verhulst
Linda Ligas
Cathy Rowland
Paul Van der Bank
Nan Williamson
Anne Woolley

PRENTICE HALL CANADA INC.

SO-DVC-353

ISBN 0-13-017062-3
© 1993 by Prentice-Hall Canada Inc., Scarborough, Ontario
ALL RIGHTS RESERVED

Anthologists: Sean Armstrong, Mary Beth Leatherdale
Researchers: Monika Croydon, Catherine Rondina

A Ligature, Inc. Book
Cover Photograph: © Galen Rowell/ Mountain Light

Canadian Cataloguing in Publication Data

Main entry under title:

Heroic Adventures: anthology

(MultiSource)
ISBN 0-13-017062-3

1. Heroes-Literary collections. 2. Children's
literature. I. Iveson, Margaret L., 1948–
II. Robinson, Sam, 1937–   . III. Series.
PZ5.H47 1993   j808.8'0353   C92–094879–0

Printed and bound in Canada

I SAW A MAN

I saw a man pursuing the horizon;
Round and round they sped.
I was disturbed at this;
I accosted the man.
"It is futile," I said,
"You can never—"
"You lie," he cried,
And ran on.

STEPHEN CRANE

Contents

MELLA

An African myth
retold by Merlin Stone

In a bright sunny clearing on the edge of a deep green forest, were the homes of reed and fiber in which the people of the village dwelled. On a mat inside one home was the father of Mella, lying close to death, while all the offerings and sacrifice, while all the music of the pipes and drums, while all the magic of Nganga healers, could not rouse him from his weakness and his dying.

Into the forest Mella walked one night, stopping in the rich moonlit dampness of the ferns, her fingertips about the crescent amulet that hung about her neck, her young woman body holding thoughts of age and sickness in its heart. There she called upon the merciful Bomu Rambi, She who watched over the village, begging for any word of what she might do to help. The leaves above her trembled with the presence of the power of the moonlight as it shone upon them, until Mella heard these words echoing over and over within her head, "You must go to the Python Healer. You must go to the Python Healer."

Mella's heart beat quickened. Her body grew cold in the warm night air. Fear crept into her worried heart. Had not her older brothers sought the help of the Python Healer many moons before and had they not fled in terror from the entrance of the python's cave, returning to the village so shaken with terror that their voices had died within their throats when they tried to speak of their visit to the Python Healer?

Lying on her straw mat in the dark of that night, Mella's eyes would not close; Mella's mind would not rest as thoughts of the Python Healer crawled in and out of her thoughts. When the dimmest rays of the morning sun fell upon her wakeful eyes, Mella rose from her mat, quickly gathered roots and grains, putting them into a small sack of elephant hide, and set off for the place that she had never been, the cave of the Python Healer, the cave set into the foothill of a mountain in the covering of the deepest, thickest jungle.

Four times the sun disappeared from the sky. Four times the sun returned to cross the heavens. All this time Mella walked through ferns as high as her head, up and down the many rock strewn hills, making her way through wooded mountainsides, sleeping in unfamiliar groves, crossing streams whose currents challenged the expert balance of her body, crossing clearings high with yellow straw that felt both soft but piercing beneath her feet, all the while bravely singing songs while her thoughts roamed between the eyes of the animals whose paths she used and anxious worry about her father, lying still and weak upon his mat at home. Then all thoughts were pushed from her mind by the sight of the spiral carved upon the rock at the entrance to the cave of the Python Healer!

In the darkness of an early evening sky, lit only by a thin crescent of the moon, Mella tried to find the voice that seemed to have fallen deep into her chest and would not rise into her throat to reach her lips—until she reminded herself of the reasons for her long journey. Taking three deep breaths of evening air, she finally called out to the hollow in the rocky cave, "I am Mella, sent to you by Bomu Rambi. I have come to ask your help, for my father has lain ill for many moons and his weakness is the weakness of my people."

Waiting in the silence for an answer, Mella noticed that even the birds had stopped their talking. They too seemed to be waiting for an answer during the time that was passing, a time that felt longer than all the days and all the nights that she had walked. And then in the darkness at the entrance of the cave, she saw a pair of eyes in the dim moonlight, heard a voice as hollow as the cave, a voice as frightening as that of Bomu Rambi had been reassuring. "The bravest of your people have fled in terror from my door. Does such a small young girl as you are have no fear that I might strangle you and leave your bones about my cave?"

"It is not a lack of fear that I possess," replied Mella to the hissing voice that seemed to be without a body, "but a love and a caring that is louder than my fear, a love and a caring for my dying father who has done no wrong, yet neither the Ngangas nor the spirits of the ancestors can rid him of the illness that lays upon him as he lies upon his mat. So deep in sorrow have I been that Bomu Rambi came in answer to my prayers. It was She who sent me to seek you out, to beg for your help if any can be given."

"Your love and caring more powerful than fear of me?" Python Healer questioned in reply. "Would you be willing to turn your back and let me crawl close to where you are standing?" Mella spoke no word but turned her back to the entrance of the cave, the pride of her people keeping her head high, though she saw only the jungle night. "Your loving and caring more powerful than your fear of me?" the Python Healer repeated, the hollow hissing voice now close behind her heels. "Would you let me twine myself about you as I might do if I chose to take you for my dinner?" Though the frantic cries of animals and birds pierced through the trees in worried, anxious warning, Mella allowed the python to wind itself about her body, and when only the legs, the arms, and the head, of what had once been Mella could be seen apart from the many rings of the python that coiled about her body, Python Healer instructed Mella to begin the long walk home.

Still she held her head up high, despite the serpent's weight upon her, despite the fear she tried to quell, until from a depth of courage in her heart, a sound rose up into her throat and floated out as song into the air so that all the animals and birds that came to gape along the path on which the serpent laden Mella walked, watched in awe of her bravery, each uttering growls or chirps of deep respect along the way. In this way exhausted Mella arrived at the edges of her village—with the Python Healer still wrapped about her body.

When the members of the village saw the monstrous creature walk into the clearing between two houses, they ran for their arrows and their spears but Mella raised her arm and called aloud, "It is Mella, inside the Python Healer! Do not harm us for I have travelled a long way to bring healing to my father." Thus they walked into the door of Mella's home, where the python soon uncoiled itself, slithering down upon the earthen floor, making its way to the mat of Mella's father.

From the small scaled pouch that hung about its neck, Mella took the healing bark as the Python Healer instructed her to do. From the small deer horn that hung about its neck, Mella took the muchonga oil as the Python Healer instructed her to do. With it she made a fire that sent the vapours of the healing bark floating into the air of their home while the Python Healer recited holy chants of the Buhera Ba Rowzi people. And then to Mella's great astonishment—her father began to kneel upon his mat, then stood erect and tall and finally began to walk about the room, something he had not done for all these many moons of illness.

Though the father spoke with many words of gratitude, providing festive food and drink for Mella and the healing serpent, the voice of the Python Healer now was silent. Once again it began to wind about the body of Mella, so that she knew she must again repeat the walk to return the Python Healer to its cave. Once again reaching the spiral marking on the entrance, Mella sighed in great relief as the python crawled down from her exhausted body and moved in silence into the darkness of its home. But as she turned to leave, the Python Healer called out and invited her to enter the deep cavern in which it lived —as animals and birds again cried out in even louder warning.

So much fear had Mella faced that once again she chanced to trust the healer who had helped her father, and step by step she made her way into the granite darkness of the cave. Suddenly a light glimmered in the distance, glowing brighter as she walked. Though she dreaded seeing broken bones lying about the cavern floor, she opened her hesitant eyes and was amazed to see pots of gold and silver, baskets of ebony and ivory and precious jewels nestled upon soft silken cloths and woven tapestries. But more astonishing than all the unexpected treasures were the words that came from Python Healer. "Take what you wish, for your courage and love should surely be rewarded."

Mella's eyes lowered with embarrassment, thinking it was she who should reward the Python Healer, and in a voice not much louder than a whisper, she asked the Python Healer to do the choosing. From a great wicker box that sat upon the rocky ground, the python quickly took a golden chain into its mouth, upon whose links was hung a golden crescent of the moon, sacred image of the Buhera Ba Rowzi, holy Ndoro emblem that matched the one that Mella always wore, the one she had touched to call upon Bomu Rambi—thus she knew that Python Healer truly was a friend.

Returning to her village, Mella told her family of the treasure of the cave, proudly showing the golden Ndoro she had won, but greed soon entered into the hearts of her brothers who began to plot the python's murder, so that they might steal the riches. Overhearing the quiet scheming voices, Mella ran quickly along the now familiar path to try to protect her friend who lived by the sign of the spiral, to warn the Python Healer of her brothers' plans—so that when the brothers arrived, they were greeted by bursts of hot, unpleasant smelling smoke, frightening thunderous roars—until they again fled in terror as they had so many moons before.

When the people of the village heard of what had happened, they sent the three boys from their home, to live alone forever in the jungle. And when in later years Mella's father died, the people of the village appointed

Mella as their leader, thus honouring her courage, her honesty and her love. Mella led the proud Buhera Ba Rowzi for all the long years of her life, visiting the Python Healer as often as she could. So it came to pass that it was Queen Mella who arranged for the great wooden carving that stood in the center of the village, a perfect likeness of the trusted Python Healer, the one who knew the magic of the Ndoro Crescent moon of Bomu Rambi —and cared for those who lived with courage, honesty and love.

Frederick Douglass: 1817–1895

Douglass was someone who,
Had he walked with wary foot
And frightened tread,
From very indecision
Might be dead,
Might have lost his soul,
But instead decided to be bold
And capture every street
On which he set his feet,
To route each path
Toward freedom's goal,
To make each highway
Choose *his* compass' choice,
To all the world cried,
Hear my voice! . . .
Oh, to be a beast, a bird,
Anything but a slave! he said.

Who would be free
Themselves must strike
The first blow, he said.

He died in 1895.
He is not dead.

LANGSTON HUGHES

The
Adventurous Life
of
JOHN GODDARD

From *The Morningside World of*
Stuart McLean

When John Goddard was fifteen years old, he sat down one night with a red pencil, a blue pen and a yellow legal pad and made a list of things he wanted to do before he died.

His list began just the way you might expect:

- Become an Eagle Scout.
- Broad jump fifteen feet.
- Make a parachute jump.
- Dive in a submarine.
- Learn ju-jitsu.

The more the boy wrote, the more his imagination took hold. The list soon left the realm of idle daydreams and entered the world of serious adolescent fantasy:

- Milk a poisonous snake.
- Light a match with a 22.
- Watch a fire-walking ceremony in Surinam.
- Watch a cremation ceremony in Bali.

And it didn't stop there. As young Goddard continued his list, his vision expanded and showed signs of the grand adventurer he was going to grow up to be:

- Explore the Amazon.
- Swim in Lake Tanganyika.
- Climb the Matterhorn.
- Retrace the travels of Marco Polo and Alexander the Great.
- Visit every country in the world.

The ideas poured onto the page and at some point took a sharp turn in tone. As Goddard added to his list, he displayed an academic sophistication well beyond his fifteen years:

- Read the works of Shakespeare, Plato, Aristotle, Dickens, Thoreau, Rousseau, Hemingway, Twain, Burroughs, Talmage, Tolstoy, Longfellow, Keats, Poe, Bacon, Whittier and Emerson.
- Become familiar with the compositions of Bach, Beethoven, Debussy, Ibert, Mendelssohn, Lalo, Milhaud, Ravel, Rimsky-Korsakov, Respighi, Rachmaninoff, Paganini, Stravinsky, Toch, Tchaikovsky, Verdi.
- Read the Bible from cover to cover.
- Play the flute and the violin.

When he put his pens down, there were 127 items on Goddard's list.

Well. Yes.

We have all taken a stab at this sort of thing at one time or another. The extraordinary difference between John Goddard and the rest of us, however, is the unsettling fact that Goddard didn't throw his list out. Nor did he chuck it into the bottom of a drawer. He kept his list in plain sight and set out to complete every item line by line. Today Goddard has check marks beside 108 of his original 127 goals. And that includes all of the items mentioned above.

Well, that's not exactly true. There are still thirty odd countries that he hasn't visited. But he is working on that.

I first read about John Goddard in *Life* magazine when I was a teenager. It was in one of those articles at the back of the magazine in a section called the "Parting Shots." The article stuck in my mind (How could I forget it?) and I always hoped I would get a chance to talk to him. Fifteen years later I sat down with his phone number in front of me and called him at his home in La Cañada, California. I wanted to talk to him, I explained, about the list I had seen so long ago in *Life*. I wanted to know if he was still working on it. Yes, he was. Did he remember what had inspired him to write it? John Goddard chuckled.

> I think what motivated me to write the list was listening to some family friends who were visiting with my parents. They had been over for dinner and were helping to clear the dishes. I was doing my homework in a little alcove, a sort of breakfast nook. The man of the family, a Dr. Keller, looked at me and said to my parents, 'I'd give anything to be John's age again. I really would do things differently. I would set out and accomplish more of the dreams of my youth.' That was the gist of his conversation—if only he could start over—and I thought, here's a man only forty-two years old, and he is feeling life has passed him by, and I thought, if I start planning now, and really work on my goals, I won't end up that way.

Almost fifty years have passed since John Goddard wrote out his life goals. He is now in his mid-sixties. But the day we spoke, he was busy preparing for a trip to the North Pole—one half of goal number 54, which is to visit both the North and the South poles. Another check mark. I spoke to John Goddard for almost two hours, and we talked about many things. I asked him if he remembered the day he wrote the list.

I remember it vividly because it was such a rite of passage for me. It was a rainy Sunday afternoon in 1941. Until that time I really hadn't crystallized all my ambitions and hopes and dreams. Writing them down was the first act in achieving them. You know, when you write something down with the sincere intent of doing it, it's a commitment. A lot of us fail to do that. We don't set deadlines and say, for example, by June of 1990 I'm going to have checked out in scuba, taken a rock climbing course and learned how to play the piano. The moment of writing it down is vivid in my mind because that was my formal commitment to that life list. And I felt I would give myself a lifetime to fulfil everything on it.

One of Goddard's early challenges was an expedition by kayak down the longest river on earth—the 4,000-mile Nile. He was the first person in the world to travel the length of the river from the headwaters to the Mediterranean. He took a bank loan to finance the trip and then paid off the loan by writing a book about his adventures. He sold the book on the lecture circuit. And that's the way he has made his living ever since. Goddard supports himself through his lectures, his books, and the sale of his films and tapes. He is not a wealthy man.

I asked him if he had ever been in any physical danger. He told me of the time he was lost in a sand storm in the Sudan, and couldn't put up a tent because the wind was blowing so hard. But he couldn't sit still because if he had stopped moving, he would have been buried alive. He told me about the time he had been shot at by river pirates in Egypt. Later I read that he had also been bitten by a rattlesnake, charged by an elephant, trapped in quicksand, been in more than one plane crash and caught in more than one earthquake.

Sometimes I go on and on about a hazardous drive my family and I had one winter between Montreal and

Toronto. It was snowing more than usual, the driving was tough, and there were a lot of cars off the road. There was also a service centre every fifty-odd miles, lots of snow-ploughs and plenty of people to help out if I had got in trouble. Nevertheless, when I tell the story of the drive I can make it sound pretty dramatic.

Imagine being able to start a story with "Exploring the Congo was difficult. . . ."

> Exploring the Congo was difficult. It took me six months and resulted in the loss of life of my partner, Jack Yowell from Kenya. Four hundred miles downstream we had a disaster when we both capsized on a raging stretch of rapids. It was the 125th set of rapids, and we were paddling fragile 60-pound, 16-foot kayaks. He got swept to the left and flipped over, and racing over to help him I got flipped over, too, and nearly drowned myself. I tried to fight to the surface and banged into the river bottom. The river was so turbulent I couldn't really tell which way the surface was, and I was drowning because I was under the water an interminable time. I think the thing that saved me was the fact that I could hold my breath for three minutes in an emergency. I was finally washed to calm water and ran along the banks desperately trying to find Jack. I couldn't see him anywhere. Then suddenly a box of matches came floating by, then his pipe, overturned kayak and aluminum paddle, but no Jack. It was very difficult to go on and travel the remaining 2,300 miles to the Atlantic. But we had promised one another if one of us did die on the upper river that the survivor would continue and finish the expedition for both of us. So I fulfilled that promise.

John Goddard still has a lot of things left on his list, but at age sixty-four he is in good shape and determined to keep at it. He does one hundred sit-ups every morning, works out on cables and weights and rides a stationary bike at least six miles a day.

I'm Nobody

I'm nobody! Who are you?
Are you nobody, too?
Then there's a pair of us—don't tell!
They'd banish us, you know.

How dreary to be somebody!
How public, like a frog
To tell your name the livelong day
To an admiring bog!

EMILY DICKINSON

On the Vanity of Earthly Greatness

The tusks that clashed in mighty brawls
Of mastodons, are billiard balls.

The sword of Charlemagne the Just
Is ferric oxide, known as rust.

The grizzly bear whose potent hug
Was feared by all, is now a rug.

Great Caesar's dead and on the shelf,
And I don't feel so well myself!

ARTHUR GUITERMAN

By the WATERS of BABYLON

A short story by
Stephen Vincent Benét

> How doth the city sit solitary, that was full of people!
> how is she become as a widow! she that was great
> among the nations, and princess among the provinces,
> how is she become tributary!
>
> *—Jeremiah, 1:1*

The north and the west and the south are good hunting ground, but it is forbidden to go east. It is forbidden to go to any of the Dead Places except to search for metal and then he who touches the metal must be a priest or the son of a priest. Afterwards, both the man and the metal must be purified. These are the rules and the laws; they are well made. It is forbidden to cross the great river and look upon the place that was the Place of the Gods—this is most strictly forbidden. We do not even say its name though we know its name. It is there that spirits live, and demons—it is there are the ashes of the Great Burning. These things are forbidden—they have been forbidden since the beginning of time.

My father is a priest; I am the son of a priest. I have been in the Dead Places near us, with my father—at first, I was afraid. When my father went into the house to search for the metal, I stood by the door and my heart felt small and weak. It was a dead man's house, a spirit house. It did not have the smell of man, though there were old bones in a corner. But it is not fitting that a priest's son should show fear. I looked at the bones in the shadow and kept my voice still.

Then my father came out with the metal—a good, strong piece. He looked at me with both eyes but I had not run away. He gave me the metal to hold—I took it and did not die. So he knew that I was truly his son and would be a priest in my time. That was when I was very young—nevertheless my brothers would not have done it, though they are good hunters. After that, they gave me the good piece of meat and the warm corner by the fire. My father watched over me—he was glad that I should be a priest. But when I boasted or wept without a reason, he punished me more strictly than my brothers. That was right.

After a time, I myself was allowed to go into the dead houses and search for metal. So I learned the ways of those houses—and if I saw bones, I was no longer afraid. The bones are light and old—sometimes they will fall into dust if you touch them. But that is a great sin.

I was taught the chants and the spells—I was taught how to stop the running of blood from a wound and many secrets. A priest must know many secrets—that was what my father said. If the hunters think we do all things by chants and spells, they may believe so—it does not hurt them. I was taught how to read in the old books and how to make the old writings—that was hard and took a long time. My knowledge made me happy—it was like a fire in my heart. Most of all, I liked to hear of the Old Days and the stories of the gods. I asked myself many questions that I could not answer, but it was good to ask them. At night, I would lie awake and listen to the wind —it seemed to me that it was the voice of the gods as they flew through the air.

We are not ignorant like the Forest People—our women spin wool on the wheel, our priests wear a white robe. We do not eat grubs from the tree, we have not forgotten the old writings, although they are hard to understand. Nevertheless, my knowledge and my lack of knowledge burned in me—I wished to know more. When I was a man at last, I came to my father and said, "It is time for me to go on my journey. Give me your leave."

He looked at me for a long time, stroking his beard, then he said at last, "Yes. It is time." That night, in the house of the priesthood, I asked for and received purification. My body hurt but my spirit was a cool stone. It was my father himself who questioned me about my dreams.

He bade me look into the smoke of the fire and see— I saw and told what I saw. It was what I have always seen—a river, and beyond it, a great Dead Place and in it the gods walking. I have always thought about that. His eyes were stern when I told him—he was no longer my father but a priest. He said, "This is a strong dream."

"It is mine," I said, while the smoke waved and my head felt light. They were singing the Star song in the outer chamber and it was like the buzzing of bees in my head.

He asked me how the gods were dressed and I told him how they were dressed. We know how they were dressed from the book, but I saw them as if they were before me. When I had finished, he threw the sticks three times and studied them as they fell.

"This is a very strong dream," he said. "It may eat you up."

"I am not afraid," I said and looked at him with both eyes. My voice sounded thin in my ears but that was because of the smoke.

He touched me on the breast and the forehead. He gave me the bow and the three arrows.

"Take them," he said. "It is forbidden to travel east. It is forbidden to cross the river. It is forbidden to go to the Place of the Gods. All these things are forbidden."

"All these things are forbidden," I said, but it was my voice that spoke and not my spirit. He looked at me again.

"My son," he said. "Once I had young dreams. If your dreams do not eat you up, you may be a great priest. If they eat you, you are still my son. Now go on your journey."

I went fasting, as is the law. My body hurt but not my heart. When the dawn came, I was out of the village. I prayed and purified myself, waiting for a sign. The sign was an eagle. It flew east.

Sometimes signs are sent by bad spirits. I waited again on the flat rock, fasting, taking no food. I was very still—I could feel the sky above me and the earth beneath. I waited till the sun was beginning to sink. Then three deer passed in the valley, going east—they did not wind me or see me. There was a white fawn with them—a very great sign.

I followed them, at a distance, waiting for what would happen. My heart was troubled about going east, yet I knew that I must go. My head hummed with my fasting—I did not even see the panther spring upon the white fawn. But, before I knew it, the bow was in my hand. I shouted and the panther lifted his head from the fawn. It is not easy to kill a panther with one arrow but the arrow went through his eye and into his brain. He died as he tried to spring—he rolled over, tearing at the ground. Then I knew I was meant to go east—I knew that was my journey. When the night came, I made my fire and roasted meat.

It is eight suns' journey to the east and a man passes by many Dead Places. The Forest People are afraid of them but I am not. Once I made my fire on the edge of a Dead Place at night and, next morning, in the dead house, I found a good knife, little rusted. That was small to what came afterward but it made my heart feel big. Always when I looked for game, it was in front of my arrow, and twice I passed hunting parties of the Forest People without their knowing. So I knew my magic was strong and my journey clean, in spite of the law.

Toward the setting of the eighth sun, I came to the banks of the great river. It was half a day's journey after I had left the god-road—we do not use the god-roads now for they are falling apart into great blocks of stone, and the forest is safer going. A long way off, I had seen the water through trees but the trees were thick. At last, I came out upon an open place at the top of a cliff. There was the great river below, like a giant in the sun. It is very long, very wide. It could eat all the streams we know and still be thirsty. Its name is Ou-dis-sun, the Sacred, the Long. No man of my tribe had seen it, not even my father, the priest. It was magic and I prayed.

Then I raised my eyes and looked south. It was there, the Place of the Gods.

How can I tell what it was like—you do not know. It was there, in the red light, and they were too big to be houses. It was there with the red light upon it, mighty and ruined. I knew that in another moment the gods would see me. I covered my eyes with my hands and crept back into the forest.

Surely, that was enough to do, and live. Surely it was enough to spend the night upon the cliff. The Forest People themselves do not come near. Yet, all through the night, I knew that I should have to cross the river and walk in the Place of the Gods, although the gods ate me up. My magic did not help me at all and yet there was a fire in my bowels, a fire in my mind. When the sun rose, I thought, 'My journey has been clean. Now I will go home from my journey." But, even as I thought so, I knew I could not. If I went to the Place of the Gods, I would surely die, but, if I did not go, I could never be at peace with my spirit again. It is better to lose one's life than one's spirit, if one is a priest and the son of a priest.

Nevertheless, as I made the raft, the tears ran out of my eyes. The Forest People could have killed me without fight, if they had come upon me then, but they did not come. When the raft was made, I said the sayings for the dead and painted myself for death. My heart was cold as a frog and my knees like water, but the burning in my mind would not let me have peace. As I pushed the raft from the shore, I began my death song—I had the right. It was a fine song.

"I am John, son of John." I sang. "My people are the Hill People. They are the men.

I go into the Dead Places but I am not slain.

I take the metal from the Dead Places but I am not blasted.

I travel upon the god-roads and am not afraid. E-yah! I have killed the panther, I have killed the fawn!

E-yah! I have come to the great river. No man has come there before.

It is forbidden to go east, but I have gone, forbidden to go on the great river, but I am there.

Open your hearts, you spirits, and hear my song.

Now I go to the Place of the Gods, I shall not return.

My body is painted for death and my limbs weak, but
my heart is big as I go to the Place of the Gods!"

All the same, when I came to the Place of Gods, I was
afraid, afraid. The current of the great river is very strong—
it gripped my raft with its hands. That was magic, for the
river itself is wide and calm. I could feel evil spirits about
me in the bright morning; I could feel their breath on my
neck as I was swept down the stream. Never have I been
so much alone—I tried to think of my knowledge, but
it was a squirrel's heap of winter nuts. There was no
strength in my knowledge any more and I felt small and
naked as a new-hatched bird—alone upon the great river,
the servant of the gods.

Yet, after a while, my eyes were opened and I saw. I
saw both banks of the river—I saw that once there had
been god-roads across it, though now they were broken
and fallen like broken vines. Very great they were, and
wonderful and broken—broken in the time of the Great
Burning when the fire fell out of the sky. And always the
current took me nearer to the Place of the Gods, and the
huge ruins rose before my eyes.

I do not know the customs of rivers—we are the People of the Hills. I tried to guide my raft with the pole but
it spun around. I thought the river meant to take me past
the Place of the Gods and out into the Bitter Water of the
legends. I grew angry then—my heart felt strong. I said
aloud, "I am a priest and the son of a priest!" The gods
heard me—they showed me how to paddle with the pole
on one side of the raft. The current changed itself—I drew
near to the Place of the Gods.

When I was very near, my raft struck and turned over.

I can swim in our lakes—I swam to the shore. There was
a great spike of rusted metal sticking out into the river—
I hauled myself up upon it and sat there, panting. I had
saved my bow and two arrows and the knife I found in
the Dead Place but that was all. My raft went whirling
downstream toward the Bitter Water. I looked after it,
and thought if it had trod me under, at least I would be
safely dead. Nevertheless, when I had dried my bowstring
and restrung it, I walked forward to the Place of the Gods.

It felt like ground underfoot; it did not burn me. It is
not true what some of the tales say, that the ground there
burns forever, for I have been there. Here and there were
the marks and stains of the Great Burning, on the ruins,
that is true. But they were old marks and old stains. It is
not true, either, what some of our priests say, that it is an
island covered with fogs and enchantments. It is not. It is
a great Dead Place—greater than any Dead Place we
know. Everywhere in it there are god-roads, though most
are cracked and broken. Everywhere there are the ruins of
the high towers of the gods.

How shall I tell what I saw? I went carefully, my
strung bow in my hand, my skin ready for danger. There
should have been the wailings of spirits and the shrieks of
demons, but there were not. It was very silent and sunny
where I had landed—the wind and the rain and the birds
that drop seeds had done their work—the grass grew in
the cracks of the broken stone. It is a fair island—no
wonder the gods built there. If I had come there, a god,
I also would have built.

How shall I tell what I saw? The towers are not all
broken—here and there one still stands, like a great tree
in a forest, and the birds nest high. But the towers themselves look blind, for the gods are gone. I saw a fish
hawk, catching fish in the river. I saw a little dance of

white butterflies over a great heap of broken stones and columns. I went there and looked about me—there was a carved stone with cut letters, broken in half. I can read letters but I could not understand these. They said UBTREAS. There was also the shattered image of a man or a god. It had been made of white stone and he wore his hair tied back like a woman's. His name was ASH-ING, as I read on the cracked half of a stone. I thought it wise to pray to ASHING, though I do not know that god.

How shall I tell what I saw? There was no smell of man left, on stone or metal. Nor were there many trees in that wilderness of stone. There are many pigeons, nesting and dropping in the towers—the gods must have loved them, or, perhaps, they used them for sacrifices. There are wild cats that roam the god-roads, green-eyed, unafraid of man. At night they wail like demons but they are not demons. The wild dogs are more dangerous, for they hunt in a pack, but them I did not meet till later. Everywhere there are carved stones, carved with magical numbers or words.

I went north—I did not try to hide myself. When a god or a demon saw me, then I would die, but meanwhile I was no longer afraid. My hunger for knowledge burned in me—there was so much that I could not understand. After a while, I knew that my belly was hungry. I could have hunted for my meat, but I did not hunt. It is known that the gods did not hunt as we do—they got their food from enchanted boxes and jars. Sometimes these are still found in the Dead Places—once, when I was a child and foolish, I opened such a jar and tasted it and found the food sweet. But my father found out and punished me for it strictly, for, often, that food is death. Now, though, I had long gone past what was forbidden, and I entered the likeliest towers, looking for the food of the gods.

I found it at last in the ruins of a great temple in the mid-city. A mighty temple it must have been, for the roof was painted like the sky at night with its stars—that much I could see, though the colors were faint and dim. It went down into great caves and tunnels—perhaps they kept their slaves there. But when I started to climb down, I heard the squeaking of rats, so I did not go—rats are unclean, and there must have been many tribes of them, from the squeaking. But near there, I found food, in the heart of a ruin, behind a door that still opened. I ate only the fruits from the jars—they had a very sweet taste. There was drink, too, in bottles of glass—the drink of the gods was strong and made my head swim. After I had eaten and drunk, I slept on the top of a stone, my bow at my side.

When I woke, the sun was low. Looking down from where I lay, I saw a dog sitting on his haunches. His tongue was hanging out of his mouth; he looked as if he were laughing. He was a big dog, with a gray-brown coat, as big as a wolf. I sprang up and shouted at him but he did not move—he just sat there as if he were laughing. I did not like that. When I reached for a stone to throw, he moved swiftly out of the way of the stone. He was not afraid of me; he looked at me as if I were meat. No doubt I could have killed him with an arrow, but I did not know if there were others. Moreover, night was falling.

I looked about me—not far away there was a great, broken god-road, leading north. The towers were high enough, but not so high, and while many of the dead houses were wrecked, there were some that stood. I went toward this god-road, keeping to the heights of the ruins, while the dog followed. When I had reached the god-road, I saw that there were others behind him. If I had slept later, they would have come upon me asleep and torn out my throat. As it was, they were sure enough of me; they did not hurry. When I went into the dead-house, they kept watch at the entrance—doubtless they thought they would have a fine hunt. But a dog cannot open a door and I knew, from the books, that the gods did not like to live on the ground but on high.

I had just found a door I could open when the dogs decided to rush. Ha! They were surprised when I shut the door in their faces—it was a good door, of strong metal. I could hear their foolish baying beyond it but I did not stop to answer them. I was in darkness—I found stairs and climbed. There were many stairs, turning around till my head was dizzy. At the top was another door—I found the knob and opened it. I was in a long small chamber—on one side of it was a bronze door that could not be opened, for it had no handle. Perhaps there was a magic word to open it but I did not have the word. I turned to the door in the opposite side of the wall. The lock of it was broken and I opened it and went in.

Within, there was a place of great riches. The god who lived there must have been a powerful god. The first room was a small anteroom—I waited there for some time, telling the spirits of the place that I came in peace and not as a robber. When it seemed to me that they had had time to hear me, I went on. Ah, what riches! Few, even, of the windows had been broken—it was all as it had been. The great windows that looked over the city had not been broken at all though they were dusty and streaked with many years. There were coverings on the floors, the colors not greatly faded, and the chairs were soft and deep. There were pictures upon the walls, very strange, very wonderful—I remember one of a bunch of flowers in a jar—if you came close to it, you could see nothing but bits of color, but if you stood away from it, the flowers might have been picked yesterday. It made my heart feel strange to look at this picture—and to look at the figure of a bird, in some hard clay, on a table and see it so like our birds. Everywhere there were books and writings, many in tongues that I could not read. The god who lived there must have been a wise god and full of knowledge. I felt I had right there, as I sought knowledge also.

Nevertheless, it was strange. There was a washing-place but no water—perhaps the gods washed in air. There was a cooking-place but no wood, and though there was a machine to cook food, there was no place to put fire in it. Nor were there candles or lamps—there were things that looked like lamps but they had neither oil nor wick. All these things were magic, but I touched them and lived—the magic had gone out of them. Let me tell one thing to show. In the washing-place, a thing said "Hot" but it was not hot to the touch—another thing said "Cold" but it was not cold. This must have been a strong magic but the magic was gone. I do not understand—they had ways—I wish that I knew.

It was close and dry and dusty in their house of the gods. I have said the magic was gone but that is not true —it had gone from the magic things but it had not gone from the place. I felt the spirits about me, weighing upon me. Nor had I ever slept in a Dead Place before—and yet, tonight, I must sleep there. When I thought of it, my tongue felt dry in my throat, in spite of my wish for knowledge. Almost I would have gone down again and faced the dogs, but I did not.

I had not gone through all the rooms when the darkness fell. When it fell, I went back to the big room looking over the city and made fire. There was a place to make fire and a box with wood in it, though I do not think they cooked there. I wrapped myself in a floor covering and slept in front of the fire—I was very tired.

Now I tell what is very strong magic. I woke in the midst of the night. When I woke, the fire had gone out and I was cold. It seemed to me that all around me there were whisperings and voices. I closed my eyes to shut them out. Some will say that I slept again, but I do not think that I slept. I could feel the spirits drawing my spirit out of my body as a fish is drawn on a line.

Why should I lie about it? I am a priest and the son of a priest. If there are spirits, as they say, in the small Dead Places near us, what spirits must there not be in that great Place of the Gods? And would not they wish to speak? After such long years? I know that I felt myself drawn as a fish is drawn on a line. I had stepped out of my body—I could see my body asleep in front of the cold fire, but it was not I. I was drawn to look out upon the city of the gods.

It should have been dark, for it was night, but it was not dark. Everywhere there were lights—lines of light—circles and blurs of light—ten thousand torches would not have been the same. The sky itself was alight—you could barely see the stars for the glow in the sky. I thought to myself, "This is strong magic," and trembled. There was a roaring in my ears like the rushing of rivers. Then my eyes grew used to the light and my ears to the sound. I knew that I was seeing the city as it had been when the gods were alive.

That was a sight indeed—yes, that was a sight: I could not have seen it in the body—my body would have died. Everywhere went the gods, on foot and in chariots—there were gods beyond number and counting and their chariots blocked the streets. They had turned night to day for their pleasure—they did not sleep with the sun. The noise of their coming and going was the noise of many waters.

It was magic what they could do—it was magic what they did.

I looked out of another window—the great vines of their bridges were mended and the god-roads went east and west. Restless, restless were the gods, and always in motion! They burrowed tunnels under rivers—they flew in the air. With unbelievable tools they did giant works— no part of the earth was safe from them, for, if they wished for a thing, they summoned it from the other side of the world. And always, as they labored and rested, as they feasted and made love, there was a drum in their ears—the pulse of the giant city, beating and beating like a man's heart.

Were they happy? What is happiness to the gods? They were great, they were mighty, they were wonderful and terrible. As I looked upon them and their magic, I felt like a child—but a little more, it seemed to me, and they would pull down the moon from the sky. I saw them with wisdom beyond wisdom and knowledge beyond knowledge. And yet not all they did was well done—even I could see that—and yet their wisdom could not but grow until all was peace.

Then I saw their fate come upon them and that was terrible past speech. It came upon them as they walked the streets of their city. I have been in fights with the Forest People—I have seen men die. But this was not like that. When gods war with gods, they use weapons we do not know. It was fire falling out of the sky and a mist that poisoned. It was the time of the Great Burning and the Destruction. They ran about like ants in the streets of their city—poor gods, poor gods! Then the towers began to fall. A few escaped—yes, a few. The legends tell it. But, even after the city had become a Dead Place, for many years the poison was still in the ground. I saw it happen, I saw the last of them die. It was darkness over the broken city and I wept.

All this, I saw. I saw it as I have told it, though not in the body. When I woke in the morning, I was hungry, but I did not think first of my hunger for my heart was perplexed and confused. I knew the reason for the Dead Places but I did not see why it had happened. It seemed to me it should not have happened, with all the magic they had. I went through the house looking for an answer. There was so much in the house I could not understand— and yet I am a priest and the son of a priest. It was like being on one side of the great river, at night, with no light to show the way.

Then I saw the dead god. He was sitting in his chair, by the window, in a room I had not entered before and, for the first moment, I thought that he was alive. Then I saw the skin on the back of his hand—it was like dry leather. The room was shut, hot and dry—no doubt that had kept him as he was. At first I was afraid to approach him—then the fear left me. He was sitting looking out over the city—he was dressed in the clothes of the gods. His age was neither young nor old—I could not tell his age. But there was wisdom in his face and great sadness. You could see that he would not have run away. He had sat at his window, watching his city die—then he himself had died. But it is better to lose one's life than one's spirit—and you could see from the face that his spirit had not been lost. I knew that if I touched him, he would fall into dust—and yet, there was something unconquered in the face.

That is all of my story, for then I knew he was a man—I knew then that they had been men, neither gods nor demons. It is a great knowledge, hard to tell and believe. They were men—they went a dark road, but they were men. I had no fear after that—I had no fear going home, though twice I fought off the dogs and once I was hunted for two days by the Forest People. When I saw my father again, I prayed and was purified. He touched my lips and my breast; he said, "You went away a boy. You come back a man and a priest." I said, "Father, they were men! I have been in the Place of the Gods and seen it! Now slay me, if it is the law—but still I know that they were men."

He looked at me out of both eyes. He said, "The law is not always the same shape—you have done what you have done. I could not have done it in my time, but you come after me. Tell!"

I told and he listened. After that, I wished to tell all the people but he showed me otherwise. He said, "Truth is a hard deer to hunt. If you eat too much truth at once, you may die of the truth. It was not idly that our fathers forbade the Dead Places." He was right—it is better the truth should come little by little. I have learned that, being a priest. Perhaps, in the old days, they ate knowledge too fast.

Nevertheless, we make a beginning. It is not for the metal alone we go to the Dead Places now—there are the books and the writings. They are hard to learn. And the magic tools are broken—but we can look at them and wonder. At least, we make a beginning. And, when I am chief priest we shall go beyond the great river. We shall go to the Place of the Gods—the place new-york— not one man but a company. We shall look for the images of the gods and find the god ASHING and the others— the gods Lincoln and Biltmore and Moses. But they were men who built the city, not gods or demons. They were men. I remember the dead man's face. They were men who were here before us. We must build again.

THE
ODYSSEY

From Robert Fitzgerald's translation
of the Greek epic poem

The Odyssey, thought to have been written by the
Greek poet Homer, is an epic poem about King
Odysseus's ten-year journey from Troy to his home in
Greece. Odysseus must overcome many obstacles, but
he eventually succeeds and returns to Ithaca where his
wife Penelope awaits him. This excerpt describes one
of his first adventures at sea.

Seventeen nights and days in the open water
he sailed, before a dark shoreline appeared;
Skhería then came slowly into view
like a rough shield of bull's hide on the sea.
But now the god of earthquake, storming home
over the mountains of Asia from the Sunburned land,
sighted him far away. The god grew sullen
and tossed his great head, muttering to himself:
"Here is a pretty cruise! While I was gone
the gods have changed their minds about Odysseus.

Look at him now, just offshore of that island
that frees him from the bondage of his exile!
Still I can give him a rough ride in, and will."

Brewing high thunderheads, he churned the deep
With both hands on his trident—called up wind
from every quarter, and sent a wall of rain
to blot out land and sea in torrential night.
Hurricane winds now struck from the South and East
shifting North West in a great spume of seas,
on which Odysseus' knees grew slack, his heart
sickened, and he said within himself:
"Rag of man that I am, is this the end of me?
I fear the goddess told it all too well—
predicting great adversity at sea
and far from home. Now all things bear her out:
the whole rondure of heaven hooded so
by Zeus in woeful cloud, and the sea raging
under such winds. I am going down, that's sure.
How lucky those Danaans were who perished
on Troy's wide seaboard, serving the Atreidai!
Would God I, too, had died there—met my end
that time the Trojans made so many casts at me
when I stood by Akhilleus after death.
I should have had a soldier's burial
and praise from the Akhaians—not this choking
waiting for me at sea, unmarked and lonely."

A great wave drove at him with toppling crest
spinning him round, in one tremendous blow,
and he went plunging overboard, the oar-haft
wrenched from his grip. A gust that came on howling
at the same instant broke his mast in two,
hurling his yard and sail far out to leeward.

Now the big wave a long time kept him under,
helpless to surface, held by tons of water,
tangled, too, by the seacloak of Kalypso.
Long, long, until he came up spouting brine,
with streamlets gushing from his head and beard;
but still bethought him, half-drowned as he was,
to flounder for the boat and get a handhold
into the bilge—to crouch there, foiling death.
Across the foaming water, to and fro,
the boat careered like a ball of tumbleweed
blown on the autumn plains, but intact still.
So the winds drove this wreck over the deep,
East Wind and North Wind, then South Wind and West,
coursing each in turn to the brutal harry.

But Ino saw him—Ino, Kadmos' daughter,
slim-legged, lovely, once an earthling girl,
now in the seas a nereid, Leukothea.
Touched by Odysseus' painful buffeting
she broke the surface, like a diving bird,
to rest upon the tossing raft and say:
"O forlorn man, I wonder
why the Earthshaker, Lord Poseidon, holds
this fearful grudge—father of all your woes.
He will not drown you, though, despite his rage.
You seem clear-headed still; do what I tell you.
Shed that cloak, let the gale take your craft,
and swim for it—swim hard to get ashore
upon Skhería, yonder,
where it is fated that you find a shelter.
Here: make my veil your sash; it is not mortal;
you cannot, now, be drowned or suffer harm.
Only, the instant you lay hold of earth,
discard it, cast it far, far out from shore

in the winedark sea again, and turn away."

After she had bestowed her veil, the nereid
dove like a gull to windward
where a dark waveside closed over her whiteness.
But in perplexity Odysseus
said to himself, his great heart laboring:
"O damned confusion! Can this be a ruse
to trick me from the boat for some god's pleasure?
No I'll not swim; with my own eyes I saw
how far the land lies that she called my shelter.
Better to do the wise thing, as I see it.
While this poor planking holds, I stay aboard;
I may ride out the pounding of the storm,
or if she cracks up, take to the water then;
I cannot think it through a better way."

But even while he pondered and decided,
the god of earthquake heaved a wave against him
high as a rooftree and of awful gloom.
A gust of wind, hitting a pile of chaff,
will scatter all the parched stuff far and wide;
just so, when this gigantic billow struck
the boat's big timbers flew apart. Odysseus
clung to a single beam, like a jockey riding,
meanwhile stripping Kalypso's cloak away;
then he slung round his chest the veil of Ino
and plunged headfirst into the sea. His hands
went out to stroke, and he gave a swimmer's kick.

But the strong Earthshaker had him under his eye,
and nodded as he said: "Go on, go on;
wander the high seas this way, take your blows
before you join that race the gods have nurtured.

Nor will you grumble, even then, I think,
for want of trouble."

Whipping his glossy team
he rode off to his glorious home at Aigai.
But Zeus's daughter Athena countered him:
she checked the course of all the winds but one,
commanding them, "Be quiet and go to sleep."
Then sent a long swell running under a norther
to bear the prince Odysseus, back from danger,
to join the Phaiákians, people of the sea.

Two nights, two days, in the solid deep-sea swell
he drifted, many times awaiting death,
until with shining ringlets in the East
the dawn confirmed a third day, breaking clear
over a high and windless sea; and mounting
a rolling wave he caught a glimpse of land.
What a dear welcome thing life seems to children
whose father, in the extremity, recovers
after some weakening and malignant illness:
his pangs are gone, the gods have delivered him.
So dear and welcome to Odysseus
the sight of land, of woodland, on that morning.

–A glossary of players and places appears on the next page.

GLOSSARY OF PLAYERS AND PLACES IN
THE ODYSSEY

Akhaians — The people of Akhaia, a region of ancient Greece

Akhilleus (Achilles) — Odysseus's fellow warrior, who was killed during the Trojan War

Athena — The patron goddess of the Greek city of Athens, protector of heroes, and daughter of Zeus

Atreidai — The Greek people who were descendants of Atreus

Danaans — The people of Artos, an ancient Greek city

Kadmos — A king of the ancient Greek city of Thebes

Kalypso — A nymph, or sea spirit, who gave Odysseus a magic cloak

Nereid — A kindly sea spirit

Odysseus — The king of the Greek city Ithaca; his journey from Troy back to his homeland is the subject of *The Odyssey*

Phaiákians — A group of splendid sailors and other people who help Odysseus

Poseidon — The god of the sea and of earthquakes and brother of Zeus; he was commonly called "Earthshaker"

Skhería — The country from which the Phaiákians came

Troy — A great city on the Aegean Sea, site of the Trojan War; also the place from which Odysseus began his journey

Zeus — The ruler of the heavens and father of other gods

The Adventurer

A ripple from an ocean rocks the boat
Rousing the sleeper
Though not enough to know if he has woken up.

He runs to the bow and cries
There I see islands. Worlds I have not yet considered.
And the wind is in the right direction.

Deep currents
Will strip my hull of weeds that cling in estuaries.
Stars not seen from shore
Will inspire new navigation.

I can pursue enemies I have never confronted
Slake appetites I do not know I have
And seek answers to questions never asked.
On giant tides I may find an understanding
To surpass all peace.

He checks the locker.
There seem supplies enough;
All the appropriate charts and instructions to mariners,
The books of Slocum, Rose and Chichester
And other solitary adventurers who had set out
And possibly even got back.

He raises the sails, scaring off the gulls.
The bow dips in submission to the wind,
The vessel surges, straining to be away.

My voyage has begun, exults the new Odysseus,
I'm free at last.
For safety he leaves just one line tied to the dock.

FRANK SMITH

Carrying
the
Running-Aways

An African-American folk tale
told by Virginia Hamilton

Never had any idea of carryin the runnin-away slaves over the river. Even though I was right there on the plantation, right by that big river, it never got in my mind to do somethin like that. But one night the woman whose house I had gone courtin to said she knew a pretty girl wanted to cross the river and would I take her. Well, I met the girl and she was awful pretty. And soon the woman was tellin me how to get across, how to go, and when to leave.

Well, I had to think about it. But each day, that girl or the woman would come around, ask me would I row the girl across the river to a place called Ripley. Well, I finally said I would. And one night I went over to the woman's house. My owner trusted me and let me come and go as I pleased, long as I didn't try to read or write anythin. For writin and readin was forbidden to slaves.

Now, I had heard about the other side of the river from the other slaves. But I thought it was just like the side where we lived on the plantation. I thought there were slaves and masters over there, too, and overseers and rawhide whips they used on us. That's why I was so scared. I thought I'd land the girl over there and some overseer didn't know us would beat us for bein out at night. They could do that, you know.

Well, I did it. Oh, it was a long rowin time in the cold, with me worryin. But pretty soon I see a light way up high. Then I remembered the woman told me to watch for a light. Told me to row to the light, which is what I did. And when I got to it, there were two men. They reached down and grabbed the girl. Then one of the men took me by the arm. Said, "You about hungry?" And if he hadn't been holdin me, I would of fell out of that rowboat.

Well, that was my first trip. I was scared for a long time after that. But pretty soon I got over it, as other folks asked me to take them across the river. Two and three at a time, I'd take them. I got used to makin three or four trips every month.

Now it was funny. I never saw my passengers after that first girl. Because I took them on the nights when the moon was not showin, it was cloudy. And I always met them in the open or in a house with no light. So I never saw them, couldn't recognize them, and couldn't describe them. But I would say to them, "What you say?" And they would say the password. Sounded like "Menare." Seemed the word came from the Bible somewhere, but I don't know. And they would have to say that word before I took them across.

Well, there in Ripley was a man named Mr. Rankins, the rest was John, I think. He had a "station" there for escaping slaves. Ohio was a free state, I found out, so once they got across, Mr. Rankins would see to them. We went at night so we could continue back for more and to be sure no slave catchers would follow us there.

Mr. Rankins had a big light about thirty feet high up and it burned all night. It meant freedom for slaves if they could get to that bright flame.

I worked hard and almost got caught. I'd been rowin fugitives for almost four years. It was in 1863 and it was a night I carried twelve runnin-aways across the river to Mr. Rankins'. I stepped out of the boat back in Kentucky and they were after me. Don't know how they found out. But the slave catchers, didn't know them, were on my trail. I ran away from the plantation and all who I knew there. I lived in the fields and in the woods. Even in caves. Sometimes I slept up in the tree branches. Or in a hay pile. I couldn't get across the river now, it was watched so closely.

Finally, I did get across. Late one night me and my wife went. I had gone back to the plantation to get her. Mr. Rankins had him a bell by this time, along with the light. We were rowin and rowin. We could see the light and hear that bell, but it seemed we weren't gettin any closer. It took forever, it seemed. That was because we were so scared and it was so dark and we knew we could get caught and never get gone.

Well, we did get there. We pulled up there and went on to freedom. It was only a few months before all the slaves was freed.

We didn't stay on at Ripley. We went on to Detroit because I wasn't takin any chances. I have children and grandchildren now. Well, you know, the bigger ones don't care so much to hear about those times. But the little ones, well, they never get tired of hearin how their grandpa brought emancipation to loads of slaves he could touch and feel in the dark but never ever see.

"Carrying the Running-Aways" is a reality tale of freedom, a true slave narrative. The former slave who first told the tale was an actual person, Arnold Gragston, a slave in Kentucky. His story of rowing runaways across the Ohio River represents thousands of such stories of escape to freedom.

The abolitionist who helped the runaways once they were across the river was John Rankin, a Presbyterian minister and a Southerner who lived in Ripley, Ohio. The town is still there, situated on the great river. A rickety wood staircase leads up Liberty Hill from Ohio River bottom lands to the Underground "station" house of the Rankin family. From 1825 to 1865, more than two thousand slaves were sheltered at the house and guided on by the family. Today, the Rankin house is a State Memorial open to the public from April through October.

Another fugitive, Levi Perry, born a slave, crossed the Ohio River into freedom with his mother about 1854. They were rescued by John Rankin and were taken in and taken care of at the house with the light. Years later, every six months or so, Levi Perry would settle his ten children around him and he would begin: "Now listen, children. I want to tell you about slavery and how my mother and I ran away from it. So you'll know and never let it happen to you." This tale was told to me recently by my mother, Etta Belle Perry Hamilton, who is 92 years old and Levi Perry's oldest daughter.

STRANGER
IN
TARANSAY

From a non-fiction story
by Farley Mowat

The village of Taransay straggles along a bleak piece of craggy shore on the outer Hebrides—those high-domed sentinels that guard the Scottish mainland coast from the driving fury of the Western Ocean. The few strangers who visit Taransay remember the acrid smell of peat smoke on the windswept hills, the tang of the dark local ale, and the sibilant patter of the Gaelic tongue spoken by the shepherds and fishermen who gather during the long evenings under the smoke-stained ceiling of the Crofter's Dram.

It is the only public house for many kilometres, and it holds within its walls the beating heart of Taransay, together with many of its memories. Strange objects hang from the narrow ceiling beams or crowd the shelves behind the bar—remembrances of ancient wrecks, flotsam of the northern seas, the trivia of time. Amongst them is a collection of tiny figures delicately carved in white bone. These are ranged in the place of honour on a centre shelf where they catch the eye and stir the mind to wonderment. There are narwhals, long-beaked and leaping from an ivory sea; walrus thrusting tiny tusks through a miniature kayak; three polar bears snarling defiance at a human figure whose upraised arm holds a sliver of a spear; and a pack of arctic wolves poised in dreadful immobility over a slaughtered muskox.

There is an alien artistry about those carvings that never sprang from the imagination of an island shepherd, yet all were carved in Taransay. They are the work of a man named Malcolm Nakusiak who was a voyager out of time.

Nakusiak's odyssey began on a July day in the mid-1800s, under a basalt cliff in a fiord on the eastern shore of Baffin Island. To the score or so of people who lived there, it was known as Auvektuk—the Walrus Place. It had no name in our language for no white man had ever visited it although each year many of them in stout wooden vessels coasted the Baffin shores chasing the bowhead whale.

These great whales were no part of men's lives at Auvektuk. For them, walrus was the staff of life. Each summer when the ice of Davis Strait came driving south, the men of Auvektuk readied spears, harpoons, and kayaks and went out into the crashing tumult of the Strait. On the grinding edges of the floes they stalked obese, tonne-weight giants that were armoured with thick hide and armed with double tusks that could rend a kayak or a man.

Of all the Auvektuk hunters, few could surpass Nakusiak. Although not yet thirty years of age, his skill and daring had become legendary. Young women smiled at him with particular warmth. And during the long winter nights Nakusiak was often the centre of a group of men who chanted the chorus as he sang his hunting songs. But Nakusiak had another skill. He was blessed with fingers that could imbue carvings made of bone and walrus ivory with the very stuff of life. Indeed, life was a full and swelling thing for Nakusiak until the July day when his pride betrayed him to the sea.

On that morning the waters of the Strait were ominously shrouded with white fog. The hunters had gathered on the shore, listening to the ludicrous fluting voices of the first walrus of the season talking together somewhere to seaward. The temptation to go after them was great, but the risk was greater. Heavy fog at that time of the year was the precursor of a westerly gale and for a kayaker to be caught in pack ice during an offshore storm was likely to be fatal. Keen as they were for walrus meat, courageous as they were, these men refused the challenge. All save one.

Gravely ignoring the caution of his fellows, Nakusiak chose to wager his strength—and his luck—against the imponderable odds of the veiled waters. The watchers on the shore saw his kayak fade into obscurity amongst the growling floes.

With visibility reduced to about the length of the kayak, Nakusiak had great difficulty locating the walrus. The heavy fog distorted their voices and confused the direction, yet he never lost track of them and, although he had already gone farther to seaward than he had intended, he still refused to give it up and turn for home. He was so tautly concerned with the hunt that he hardly noticed the rising keen of the west wind. . . .

Some days later, and nearly three hundred kilometres to the southeast, a Norwegian whaler was pounding its way southward through Davis Strait. The dirty, ice-scarred wooden ship was laden to the marks with oil and baleen. The crewmen were driving toward the hoped-for freedom of the open seas, all sails set and drawing taut in the brisk westerly that was the last vestige of a nor'west gale.

In the crow's-nest the ice-watch swung his telescope, searching for leads. He glimpsed something on a distant floe off the port bow. Taking it to be a polar bear, he bellowed a change of course to the helmsman on the poop. Men began to scurry across the decks, some running for guns while others climbed partway up the shrouds to better vantage points. The ship shouldered its way through the pack toward the object on the ice and the crew watched with heightened interest as it resolved itself into the shape of a man slumped on the crest of a pressure ridge.

The ship swung into the wind, sails slatting as two seamen scampered across the moving ice, hoisted the limp body of Nakusiak in their arms and danced their way back from floe to floe, while a third man picked up the Inuit's broken kayak and brought it to the ship as well.

The whalers were rough men, but a castaway is a castaway no matter what his race or colour. They gave Nakusiak schnapps*, and when he was through choking they gave him hot food, and soon he began to recover from his ordeal on the drifting ice. All the same, his first hours aboard the ship were a time of bewilderment and unease. Although he had seen whaling ships in the distance and had heard many barely credible stories from other Inuit about the Kablunait—the Big Ears—who hunted the bowhead, he had never before been on a ship or seen a white man with his own eyes.

He began to feel even more disturbed as the whaler bore steadily toward the southeast, completely out of sight of land, carrying him away from Auvektuk. He had been hoping the ship would come about and head north and

---

*schnapps   a strong liquor (German)

west along the coast into the open water frequented by the bowheads, but it failed to do so, and his efforts to make the Kablunait realize that he must go home availed him nothing. When the ship reached open water, rounded Kap Farvel at the south tip of Greenland, and bore away almost due east, Nakusiak became frantic. Feverishly he began repairing his kayak with bits of wood and canvas given to him by the ship's carpenter, but he worked so obviously that he gave away his purpose. The newly patched kayak was taken from him and lashed firmly to the top of the after hatch where it was always under the eye of the helmsman and the officer on watch. The whalers acted as they did to save Nakusiak's life, for they believed he would surely perish if he put out into the wide ocean in such a tiny craft. Because he came of a race that accepted what could not be altered, Nakusiak ceased to contemplate escape. He had even begun to enjoy the voyage, when the terrible winds of his own land caught up to him again.

The whaler was southeast of the Faeroe Islands when another ice-born nor'west gale struck. It was a stout ship and ran ably before the gale, rearing and plunging on the following seas. When some of the double-reefed sails began to blow out with the noise of cannon fire, the crew stripped the ship down to bare poles; and when the massive rollers threatened to poop it, they broke out precious cases of whale oil, smashed them open, and let the oil run out of the scuppers to smother the pursuing greybeards.

The ship would have endured the storm had not the mainmast shrouds, worn thin by too many seasons in the ice, suddenly let go. They parted with a wicked snarl and in the same instant the mainmast snapped like a broken bone and thundered over the lee side. Tethered by a maze of lines, the broken spar acted like a sea anchor and the ship swung inexorably around into the trough . . . broached, and rolled half over.

There was no time to launch the whaleboats. The great seas tramped over them, snatching them away. There was barely time for Nakusiak to grab his knife, cut the kayak loose, and wriggle into the narrow cockpit before another giant comber thundered down upon the decks and everything vanished under a welter of water.

Washed clear, Nakusiak and the kayak hung poised for a moment on the back of a mountainous sea. The Inuit held his breath as he slipped down a slope so steep it seemed to him it must lead to the very bowels of the ocean. But the kayak was almost weightless, and it refused to be engulfed by the sucking seas. Sometimes it seemed to leap free and, like a flying fish, be flung from crest to crest. Sometimes it slipped completely over, but when this happened, Nakusiak, hanging head down beneath the surface, was able to right his little vessel with the twisting double paddle. He had laced the sealskin skirt sewn to the cockpit coaming so tightly around his waist that no water could enter the vessel. Man and kayak were one indivisible whole. The crushing strength of the ocean could not prevail against them.

The bit of arctic flotsam, with its human heart, blew into the southeast for so long a time that Nakusiak's eyes blurred into sightlessness. His ears became impervious to the roar of water. His muscles cracked and twisted in agony. And then, as brutally as it had begun, the ordeal ended.

A mighty comber lifted the kayak in curling fingers and flung it high on the roaring shingle of a beach where it shattered like an egg. Although he was half stunned, Nakusiak managed to crawl clear and drag himself above the storm tide line.

Hours later he was awakened from the stupor of exhaustion by the cries of swooping, black-backed gulls. His vision had cleared, but his brain remained clouded by the strangeness of what lay around him. The great waves rolled in from the sounding sea but nowhere on their heaving surface was there the familiar glint of ice. Flocks of sea birds that were alien both in sound and form hung threateningly above him. A massive cliff of a dull red hue reared high above the narrow beach. In the crevices of the cliff outlandish flowers bloomed, and vivid green turf such as he had never seen before crested the distant headlands.

The headlands held his gaze for there was something on them which gave him a sense of the familiar. Surely, he thought, those white patches on the high green places must be scattered drifts of snow. He stared intently until fear shattered the illusion. The white things moved! They lived! And they were innumerable! Nakusiak scuttled up the beach to the shelter of a water-worn cave, his heart pounding. He knew only one white beast of comparable size—the arctic wolf—and he could not credit the existence of wolves in such numbers . . . if, indeed, the things he had seen were only wolves, and not something even worse.

For two days Nakusiak hardly dared to leave the cave. He satisfied his thirst with water dripping from the rocks, and tried to ease his hunger with oily-tasting seaweed. By the third day he had become desperate enough to explore the cliff-locked beach close to his refuge. He had two urgent needs: food . . . and a weapon. He found a one-metre length of driftwood and a few minutes' work sufficed for him to lash his knife to it. Armed with this crude spear his courage began to return. He also found food of sorts: a handful of shellfish and some small fishes that had been trapped in a tidal pool. But there were not enough of these to more than take the edge off his growing hunger.

On the morning of the fourth day he made his choice. Whatever alien world this was that he had drifted to, he would no longer remain in hiding to endure starvation. He determined to leave the sterile little beach and chance whatever lay beyond the confining cliffs.

It was a long and arduous climb up the red rock wall and he was bone weary by the time he clawed his way over the grassy lip to sprawl, gasping for breath, on the soft turf. But his fatigue washed out of him instantly when, not more than a hundred paces away, he saw a vast assemblage of the mysterious white creatures. Nakusiak clutched the spear and his body became rigid.

The sheep, with the curiosity characteristic of members of their family, were intrigued by the fur-clad figure on the rim of the cliff. Slowly the flock approached, led by a big ram with black, spiralled horns. Some of the ewes shook their heads and bleated, and in this action the Inuit saw the threat of a charge.

The sheep bleated in a rising chorus and shuffled a few steps closer.

Nakusiak reached his breaking point. He charged headlong into the white mob, screaming defiance as he came. The sheep stood stupidly for a moment, then wheeled and fled, but already he was among them, thrusting fiercely with his makeshift spear.

The startled flock streamed away leaving Nakusiak, shaking as with a fever, to stare down at the two animals he had killed. That they were mortal beings, not spirits, he could no longer doubt. Wild with relief he began to laugh, and as the sound of his shrill voice sent the remaining sheep scurrying even farther into the rolling distance, Nakusiak unbound his knife and was soon filling his starving belly with red meat—and finding it to his taste.

That strange scene under the pallid Hebridean sky had been witnessed by the gulls, the sheep, . . . and by one other. Atop a ridge a half-kilometre inland a sharp-faced, tough-bodied man of middle age had seen the brief encounter. Angus Macrimmon had been idly cleaning the dottle from his pipe when his practised shepherd's glance had caught an unaccustomed movement from the flock. He looked up and his heavy brows drew together in surprise as he saw the sheep converging on a shapeless, unidentifiable figure lying at the edge of the cliff. Before Macrimmon could do more than get to his feet he saw the shape rise— squat, shaggy, and alien—and fling itself screaming on the flock. Macrimmon saw the red glare of blood against white fleece and watched the killer rip open a dead sheep and begin to feed on the raw flesh.

The Hebrideans live close to the ancient world of their ancestors, and although there are kirks* enough on the Islands, many beliefs linger on that owe nothing to the Christian faith. When Macrimmon watched the murder of his sheep, he was filled not only with anger but with dread, for he could not credit that the thing he saw was human.

Cursing himself for having left his dog at home, the shepherd went for help, running heavily toward the distant village. He was breathless by the time he reached it. Armed with whatever they could find, a dozen men were soon gathered together, calling their dogs about them. Two of them carried muzzle-loading shotguns while another carried a long-barrelled military musket.

The day was growing old when they set out across the moors, but the light was still clear. From afar the shepherds saw the white flecks that were the two dead sheep.

---

*kirk   church (Scottish)

Grouped close, they went forward cautiously until one of them raised an arm and pointed, and they all saw the shaggy thing that crouched beside one of the sheep.

They set the dogs on it.

Nakusiak had been so busy slicing up meat to sun-dry in the morning that he did not notice the approaching shepherds until the frenzied outcry of the dogs made him look up. He had never before seen dogs like these and he had no way of knowing that they were domestic beasts. He sprang to his feet and stood uncertainly, eyes searching for a place of refuge. Then his glance fell on the grim mob of approaching shepherds and he sensed their purpose as surely as a fox senses the purpose of the hunters.

Now the dogs were on him. The leader, a rangy black-and-brown collie, made a circling lunge at this strange-smelling, strangely clad figure standing bloody-handed beside the torn carcasses. Nakusiak reacted with a two-handed swing of the spear-shaft, striking the dog so heavily on the side of its head that he broke its neck. There was a hubbub among the shepherds, then one of them dropped to his knee and raised the long musket.

The remaining dogs closed in again and Nakusiak backed to the very lip of the cliff, swinging the shaft to keep them off. He lifted his head to the shepherds and in an imploring voice cried out: "*Inukuala eshuinak!* It is a man who means no harm!"

For answer came the crash of the gun. The ball struck him in the left shoulder and the force of the blow spun him around so that he lost his balance. There was a shout from the shepherds and they rushed forward, but they were still a hundred metres away when Nakusiak stumbled over the cliff edge.

There was luck in the thing, for he only fell free a few metres before bringing up on a rocky knob. Scrabbling frantically with his right hand he managed to cling to the steep slope and slither another metre or so past a slight overhang until he could lie, trembling and spent, on a narrow ledge undercut into the wall of rock.

When the men joined the hysterical dogs peering over the cliff edge, there was nothing to be seen except the glitter of waves on the narrow beach far below and the flash of gulls disturbed from their resting places.

The shepherds were oddly silent. They were hearing again that despairing cry, instantly echoed by the shot. Whatever the true identity of the sheep-killer might be, they knew in their hearts that he was human, and the knowledge did not sit easily with them.

They shifted uncomfortably until the man who had fired spoke up defiantly.

"Whatever 'twas, 'tis gone now surely," he said. "And 'tis as well, for look you at the way it tore the sheep and killed the dog!"

The others glanced at the dead dog and sheep, but they had nothing to say until Macrimmon spoke.

"Would it not be as well, do you think, to make a search of the beach?"

"Ach, man, don't be daft!" the gunner replied irritably. " 'Twould be the devil's own job to gang* down there . . . and for what? If that thing was alive when it fell, then 'tis certain dead enough now. And if 'twas never alive at all . . ." He let the sentence lie unfinished.

Calling the dogs, the shepherds moved homeward over the darkening moors, and each one wrestled with his doubts in silence.

There was no police officer at Taransay, and no one offered to carry a message to the nearest constable across

---

*gang   go (Scottish)

the mountains in distant Stornoway. Macrimmon put the feelings of all the men into words when he was being questioned about the event by his wife and daughters.

"What's done is done. There's no good to come from telling the wide world what's to be found on the moors, for they'd no believe it. Best let it be forgotten."

Yet Macrimmon himself could not forget. During the next two days and nights he found himself haunted by the memory of that alien voice. Up on the inland moors sloping to the mountain peaks, the wind seemed to echo it. The cry of the gulls seemed to echo it. It beat into the hard core of the man and would not be silenced and, in the end, it prevailed.

On the third morning he stood once more at the edge of the cliff . . . and cursed himself for a fool. Nevertheless, that dour and weatherbeaten man carefully lowered himself over the cliff edge. His dog wheened unhappily but dared not follow as his master disappeared from view.

The tide was driving out and the shingle glistened wetly far below him, but the shepherd did not look down. He worked his way skilfully, for in his youth he had been a great one at finding and carrying off the eggs of the cliff-nesting gulls. However he was no youth now and before he had descended halfway he was winded and his hands were cut and bruised. He found a sloping ledge that ran diagonally toward the beach and he was feeling his way along it when he passed close to a late-nesting gannet. The huge bird flung herself outward, violently flailing the air. A wing struck sharply against Macrimmon's face and involuntarily he raised a hand to fend her off. In that instant the shale on which his feet were braced crumbled beneath him and he was falling away toward the waiting stones.

Unseen on the cliff top, the dog sensed tragedy and howled.

The dog's howl awakened Nakusiak from fevered sleep in the protection of the little cave which had been his first sanctuary. Here, on a bed of seaweed, he lay waiting for his body to heal itself. His swollen shoulder throbbed almost unbearably but he stolidly endured, for it was in his nature to endure. All the same, as he waited for time to work for him, he was conscious that there was nothing ahead in this alien world but danger and ultimate destruction.

When the dog's howl woke him, Nakusiak shrank farther into the recesses of his cave. His good hand clutched the only weapon left to him . . . a lump of barnacle-encrusted rock. He lifted it and held it poised as the rattle of falling stones mingled with a wailing human shout outside his cave.

His heart beat heavily in the silence that followed. It was a silence that reminded Nakusiak of how it is when an ermine has cornered a ground squirrel in a rock pile and waits unseen for the trapped beast to venture out. Nakusiak was aware of anger rising above his pain. Was he not *Inuk*—a Person—and was a person to be treated as a beast? He changed his grip on the rock, then, with a shout of defiance, stumbled out of his sanctuary into the morning light.

The sun momentarily blinded him and he stood tensely waiting for the attack he was sure would come. There was no sound . . . no motion. The glare eased and he stared about him. On a thick windrow of seaweed a few metres away he saw the body of a man lying face down, blood oozing from a rent in his scalp.

Nakusiak stared at this, his enemy, and his heart thudded furiously as the inert body seemed to stir, and mumbled sounds came from its mouth. In an instant Nakusiak was standing over the shepherd, the lump of rock raised high. Death hovered over Angus Macrimmon, and only a miracle could have averted it. A miracle took place. It was the miracle of pity.

Nakusiak slowly lowered his arm. He stood trembling, looking down at the wounded man and the trickle of blood from the deep wound. Then with his good arm Nakusiak gripped the shepherd, rolled him over, and laboriously dragged his enemy up the shingle to the shelter of the cave.

A search party found the dog on the cliff edge the next morning and guessed grimly at what had happened. But the searchers only guessed a part of it. When a couple of hours later six of them, all well armed, reached the beach in a fishing skiff, they were totally unprepared for what they found.

A thin curl of smoke led them directly to the cave. When they came to peer fearfully into the narrow cleft, guns at the ready, their faces showed such baffled incredulity at the scene before them that Macrimmon could not forbear smiling.

"Dinna be frighted, lads," he said from the seaweed mattress where he lay. "They's none here but us wild folk and we'll no eat you."

Inside the cave a small driftwood fire, kindled by Nakusiak with Macrimmon's flint and steel, burned smokily. The shepherd's head was bound with strips of his own shirt, but his bruised back with its broken ribs was covered with the fur parka that had been on the back of the sheepstealer not long since. Beside him, staring uneasily at the newcomers, Nakusiak sat bare to the waist, hugging his wounded shoulder with his good arm.

The Inuit glanced nervously from Macrimmon's smiling face to the blob of heads crammed into the cave entrance, then slowly he too began to smile. It was the inexpressibly relieved grin of one who has been lost in a frightful void and who has come back into the land of humans.

For many days Nakusiak and Macrimmon lay in adjoining beds in the shepherd's cottage while their wounds healed. Macrimmon's wife and daughters gave the Inuit care and compassion, for they acknowledged their debt to him. For his part, he entertained them with songs in Inuit, at which the good wife muttered under her breath about "outlandish things," but smiled warmly at the stranger for all of that.

As he was accepted by the Macrimmons, so was he accepted by the rest of the villagers, for they were kindly people and they were also greatly relieved that they did not have to bear the sin of murder. Within a few weeks the Inuit was being referred to with affection by all and sundry, as "the queer wee laddie who came out of the sea."

Nakusiak soon adjusted to the Hebridean way of life, having accepted the fact that he would never be able to return to his own land. He learned to speak the language, and he became a good shepherd, a superb hunter of sea fowl and grey seals, and a first-rate fisherman as well. Three years after his arrival at Taransay, he married Macrimmon's eldest daughter and started a family of his own, taking the Christian name of Malcolm at the insistence of the young local clergyman who was one of those who particularly befriended him. During the long winter evenings he would join the other men at the Crofter's Dram and there, sitting before the open fire, would whittle his marvellous little carvings as a way of describing to his companions the life he had known in the distant land of the Inuit.

The Man
Who Killed
the Sea Monster

An Inuit legend
retold by Ramona Maher

On Kodiak Island lived a young man. He was a good hunter and trapper on land, and with his dip net and spear he caught many fish. But most of all, the young man wanted to stand in the front of a kayak with a harpoon when the men of the island went out to the deep water for whales and seals.

The young man spent many long hours practicing with his harpoon. He would harpoon floating logs, and with each throw the harpoon landed, quivering, in the log.

But when the young man went to the old men of the village, to ask whether he could be part of the seal-hunting kayaks, the old men would shake their heads. "No, your father brought bad luck to the village. He harpooned a giant whale, one that was too large for the kayak he was in. The whale pulled the kayak out to sea. Five men of our village were lost."

"I will not be careless," said the young man. "Please let me go." He showed them how he could send his harpoon into a target, straight as a sinew.

The old men still shook their heads. "Yes, you are a good hunter, but you would bring us bad luck out on the sea. Hunt bears here on the island with your bow and arrow. In that way you can be of the most service to your village."

The young man did as the elders told him to do. He killed the giant bears that roamed the island. When he took one of the bears back to his village there was great feasting.

The young man would not be happy at the feast and the ceremonies. More than anything else, he still wanted to be a harpooner in a kayak.

One day the men set out in their kayaks to go after fur seals. Their kayaks did not get out of the bay. The young man and the women and children of the village stood on the shore, watching the kayaks shoot swiftly through the water, back to the village.

"What is wrong?" called the young man.

The women groaned as they saw in one of the kayaks the lifeless-seeming body of a man.

"A monster," the man was muttering. "A whale with the face of a dog!"

One of the rowers told the young man what had happened. "A great fish, almost like a whale, will not let the boats out of the bay. He lashed with his powerful tail fin and broke up the kayak in which that man was rowing. The harpooner in that boat went under the water, and we never saw him come up again."

A whale with the face of a dog! What could that be? wondered the young man.

The next day, several kayaks ventured out from the village. In less than half an hour the kayaks came nudging back at the shore.

"The whale will not let us get out of the bay," said one of the kayak men. "He means to keep us from harpooning the killer whales or catching the seals."

Each day one or two kayaks went out in the bay to see if they could slip past the whale with the face of a dog. Each day it was useless. The men just sat around the village, in the sweathouse, talking and trying to think of ways to outwit the monster whale.

No one had any ideas. They were all afraid, thought the young man, because they remembered the harpooner who had been lost and the rower whose legs had been paralyzed by the great whale's tail fin.

The young man stood on the highest cliff in the island and looked out to the mouth of the bay. He could see a black object, swimming powerfully around. He saw a spout rise from a blowhole on the creature's back, and he knew it was the monster whale.

"I will come after you, whale," promised the young man. "If I harpoon you, I will be the bravest hunter in the village."

He kept his plan a secret. Dragging his kayak into the trees off the beach, he painted one side of it red. The other side he painted black. With white paint, he painted a crab on the left side of the bow. With yellow paint, he painted a human hand on the right side of the bow. Then he took blue paint and went to the stern of the boat. He painted a blue star on the left side of the stern, and he painted a blue kayak on the right side of the stern.

Then, using a small twig which he broke off a tree as a brush, he painted the same objects on his left hand. He used red paint. He painted a star on his thumb. On the first finger of his left hand he painted a kayak. On the second finger of his left hand he painted a crab, and on his third finger he painted a tiny hand with five fingers.

When the paint had dried, the young man took his harpoon and climbed into the kayak. He sat down on the matting of moss and sticks in the bed of the kayak and began to row. The harpoon lay near him so that he could grasp it quickly.

No one from the village had seen him depart. Out into the bay, farther and farther, the young man rowed. Halfway out, he began to look anxiously for the whale with the face of a dog. It was nowhere in sight.

He kept on rowing. Then the whale rose up beside his kayak, shooting a terrible fountain of water out of the blowhole. The spout was so high it almost hid the sun from sight.

The kayak rocked and almost rolled over, but the young man stood upright and steadied it with his feet. The whale with the face of a dog had made a great circle around the small kayak and was coming toward him, head on. The young man wanted to hide his face from the hideous, red-eyed glare of the great fish.

But he managed to keep his eyes fixed on the whale's eyes. He had the feeling he was safe as long as he kept his gaze fastened directly on the whale.

He began to row slowly back and forth, in front of the whale. First he rowed so that the red side of the kayak faced the monster; then he rowed so that the black side showed.

"Do you see that crab, oh whale?"

The whale had a voice like the snarling of a hundred dogs. "I see the crab."

"Do you see the human hand, oh whale?"

"I see the human hand painted on your frail boat," said the whale.

"Do you see the kayak painted on the stern of the boat?" asked the young man.

"Yes," snarled the whale. He made as if to lower his head and charge the kayak.

The young man raised his voice. "Do you see the star painted on the stern of the boat, oh whale?"

A jet of water came from the blowhole of the whale, as if he were laughing. "I smash through stars every night, in the water. I shall smash my way through your star also."

"Wait." The young man held up his hand so that the whale could see the same figures painted on it. At the same time, his right hand tightened around the harpoon.

"The crab means that you are powerless against the power of the sea," said the young man bravely. "You are powerless against the power of man—that is the reason for the human hand painted on the boat. You are weak before the power from above—that is the power of the star which I have brought with me."

The eyes of the whale with the face of a dog grew redder. "What is the meaning of the kayak sign?"

"The power of man, the power of the sea, and the power from above—all these can seize and kill you," said the young man. "And the kayak has the power to tow you to land."

With a great bellow, the whale headed for the kayak. With great skill, the young man rowed the craft to one side of the whale as it attacked. As the broad back of the fish passed him, he launched his harpoon into the whale's brain.

Then he held on tightly. The great whale had charged so powerfully that the kayak was being pulled toward shore, towed by the rope of the harpoon which was thrust deep in the whale's body.

The creature crashed on the beach, about a mile from the village. The young man crawled out of his kayak and sloshed ashore to view the monster he had captured. It was a great and ugly creature, with the fangs and face of a dog.

The villagers had felt the shock of the great whale's body as it slid up on the beach. They streamed down the shore to view the monster.

"This looks like the whale that towed your father's boat out to sea," said an old man, who was so old he knew all the village's history.

One of the most respected sea hunters took the young man's harpoon and put it in his kayak, a sign that he was asking the young man to join his crew.

The young man became one of the best and most honored hunters on Kodiak Island. Always, when he went out to hunt seals or whales, his boat was decorated with a crab and a hand on the bow, a star and a kayak on the stern.

All this happened a long time ago. But the Kodiak hunters still rely on good luck from the sea and the heavens and on their skill with the harpoon and kayak. These things bring them home safely with a good catch.

FIFTY-FIRST
DRAGON

A short story from the book
Seeing Things at Night
by Heywood Broun

Of all the pupils at the knight school Gawaine le Cœur-Hardy was among the least promising. He was tall and sturdy, but his instructors soon discovered that he lacked spirit. He would hide in the woods when the jousting class was called, although his companions and members of the faculty sought to appeal to his better nature by shouting to him to come out and break his neck like a man. Even when they told him that the lances were padded, the horses no more than ponies and the field unusually soft for late autumn, Gawaine refused to grow enthusiastic. The Headmaster and the Assistant Professor of Pleasaunce were discussing the case one spring afternoon and the Assistant Professor could see no remedy but expulsion.

"No," said the Headmaster, as he looked out at the purple hills which ringed the school, "I think I'll train him to slay dragons."

"He might be killed," objected the Assistant Professor.

"So he might," replied the Headmaster brightly, but he added, more soberly, "we must consider the greater good. We are responsible for the formation of this lad's character."

"Are the dragons particularly bad this year?" interrupted the Assistant Professor. This was characteristic. He always seemed restive when the head of the school began to talk ethics and the ideals of the institution.

"I've never known them worse," replied the Headmaster. "Up in the hills to the south last week they killed a number of peasants, two cows and a prize pig. And if this dry spell holds there's no telling when they may start a forest fire simply by breathing around indiscriminately."

"Would any refund on the tuition fee be necessary in case of an accident to young Cœur-Hardy?"

"No," the principal answered, judicially, "that's all covered in the contract. But as a matter of fact he won't be killed. Before I send him up in the hills I'm going to give him a magic word."

"That's a good idea," said the Professor. "Sometimes they work wonders."

From that day on Gawaine specialized in dragons. His course included both theory and practice. In the morning there were long lectures on the history, anatomy, manners and customs of dragons. Gawaine did not distinguish himself in these studies. He had a marvelously versatile gift for forgetting things. In the afternoon he showed to better advantage, for then he would go down to the South Meadow and practise with a battle-ax. In this exercise he was truly impressive, for he had enormous strength as well as speed and grace. He even developed a deceptive display of ferocity. Old alumni say that it was a thrilling sight to see Gawaine charging across the field toward the dummy paper dragon which had been set up for his practice. As he ran he would brandish his ax and shout, "A murrain on thee!" or some other vivid bit of campus slang. It never took him more than one stroke to behead the dummy dragon.

Gradually his task was made more difficult. Paper gave way to papier mâché and finally to wood, but even the toughest of these dummy dragons had no terrors for Gawaine. One sweep of the ax always did the business. There were those who said that when the practice was protracted until dusk and the dragons threw long, fantastic shadows across the meadow Gawaine did not charge so impetuously nor shout so loudly. It is possible there was malice in this charge. At any rate, the Headmaster decided by the end of June that it was time for the test. Only the night before a dragon had come close to the school grounds and had eaten some of the lettuce from the garden. The faculty decided that Gawaine was ready. They gave him a diploma and a new battle-ax and the Headmaster summoned him to a private conference.

"Sit down," said the Headmaster. "Have a cigarette."
Gawaine hesitated.

"Oh, I know it's against the rules," said the Headmaster. "But after all, you have received your preliminary degree. You are no longer a boy. You are a man. Tomorrow you will go out into the world, the great world of achievement."

Gawaine took a cigarette. The Headmaster offered him a match, but he produced one of his own and began to puff away with a dexterity which quite amazed the principal.

"Here you have learned the theories of life," continued the Headmaster, resuming the thread of his discourse, "but after all, life is not a matter of theories. Life is a matter of facts. It calls on the young and the old alike to face these facts, even though they are hard and sometimes unpleasant. Your problem, for example, is to slay dragons."

"They say that those dragons down in the south wood are five hundred feet long," ventured Gawaine, timorously.

"Stuff and nonsense!" said the Headmaster. "The curate saw one last week from the top of Arthur's Hill. The dragon was sunning himself down in the valley. The curate didn't have an opportunity to look at him very long because he felt it was his duty to hurry back to make a report to me. He said the monster, or shall I say, the big lizard?—wasn't an inch over two hundred feet. But the size has nothing at all to do with it. You'll find the big ones even easier than the little ones. They're far slower on their feet and less aggressive, I'm told. Besides, before you go I'm going to equip you in such fashion that you need have no fear of all the dragons in the world."

"I'd like an enchanted cap," said Gawaine.

"What's that?" answered the Headmaster, testily.

"A cap to make me disappear," explained Gawaine.

The Headmaster laughed indulgently. "You mustn't believe all those old wives' stories," he said. "There isn't any such thing. A cap to make you disappear, indeed! What would you do with it? You haven't even appeared yet. Why, my boy, you could walk from here to London, and nobody would so much as look at you. You're nobody. You couldn't be more invisible than that."

Gawaine seemed dangerously close to a relapse into his old habit of whimpering. The Headmaster reassured him: "Don't worry; I'll give you something much better than an enchanted cap. I'm going to give you a magic word. All you have to do is to repeat this magic charm once and no dragon can possibly harm a hair of your head. You can cut off his head at your leisure."

He took a heavy book from the shelf behind his desk and began to run through it. "Sometimes," he said, "the charm is a whole phrase or even a sentence. I might, for instance, give you 'To make the'—No, that might not do. I think a single word would be best for dragons."

"A short word," suggested Gawaine.

"It can't be too short or it wouldn't be potent. There isn't so much hurry as all that. Here's a splendid magic word: 'Rumplesnitz.' Do you think you can learn that?"

Gawaine tried and in an hour or so he seemed to have the word well in hand. Again and again he interrupted the lesson to inquire, "And if I say 'Rumplesnitz' the dragon can't possibly hurt me?" And always the Headmaster replied, "If you only say 'Rumplesnitz,' you are perfectly safe."

Toward morning Gawaine seemed resigned to his career. At daybreak the Headmaster saw him to the edge of the forest and pointed him to the direction in which he should proceed. About a mile away to the southwest a cloud of steam hovered over an open meadow in the woods and the Headmaster assured Gawaine that under the steam he would find a dragon. Gawaine went forward slowly. He wondered whether it would be best to approach the dragon on the run as he did in his practice in the South Meadow or to walk slowly toward him, shouting "Rumplesnitz" all the way.

The problem was decided for him. No sooner had he come to the fringe of the meadow than the dragon spied him and began to charge. It was a large dragon and yet it seemed decidedly aggressive in spite of the Headmaster's statement to the contrary. As the dragon charged it released huge clouds of hissing steam through its nostrils.

It was almost as if a gigantic teapot had gone mad. The dragon came forward so fast and Gawaine was so frightened that he had time to say "Rumplesnitz" only once. As he said it, he swung his battle-ax and off popped the head of the dragon. Gawaine had to admit that it was even easier to kill a real dragon than a wooden one if only you said "Rumplesnitz."

Gawaine brought the ears home and a small section of the tail. His school mates and the faculty made much of him, but the Headmaster wisely kept him from being spoiled by insisting that he go on with his work. Every clear day Gawaine rose at dawn and went out to kill dragons. The Headmaster kept him at home when it rained, because he said the woods were damp and unhealthy at such times and that he didn't want the boy to run needless risks. Few good days passed in which Gawaine failed to get a dragon. On one particularly fortunate day he killed three, a husband and wife and a visiting relative. Gradually he developed a technique. Pupils who sometimes watched him from the hill-tops a long way off said that he often allowed the dragon to come within a few feet before he said "Rumplesnitz." He came to say it with a mocking sneer. Occasionally he did stunts. Once when an excursion party from London was watching him he went into action with his right hand tied behind his back. The dragon's head came off just as easily.

As Gawaine's record of killings mounted higher the Headmaster found it impossible to keep him completely in hand. He fell into the habit of stealing out at night and engaging in long drinking bouts at the village tavern. It was after such a debauch that he rose a little before dawn one fine August morning and started out after his fiftieth dragon. His head was heavy and his mind sluggish. He was heavy in other respects as well, for he had adopted the somewhat vulgar practice of wearing his medals, ribbons and all, when he went out dragon hunting. The decorations began on his chest and ran all the way down to his abdomen. They must have weighed at least eight pounds.

Gawaine found a dragon in the same meadow where he had killed the first one. It was a fair-sized dragon, but evidently an old one. Its face was wrinkled and Gawaine thought he had never seen so hideous a countenance. Much to the lad's disgust, the monster refused to charge and Gawaine was obliged to walk toward him. He whistled as he went. The dragon regarded him hopelessly, but craftily. Of course it had heard of Gawaine. Even when the lad raised his battle-ax the dragon made no move. It knew that there was no salvation in the quickest thrust of the head, for it had been informed that this hunter was protected by an enchantment. It merely waited, hoping something would turn up. Gawaine raised the battle-ax and suddenly lowered it again. He had grown very pale and he trembled violently. The dragon suspected a trick. "What's the matter?" it asked, with false solicitude.

"I've forgotten the magic word," stammered Gawaine.

"What a pity," said the dragon. "So that was the secret. It doesn't seem quite sporting to me, all this magic stuff, you know. Not cricket, as we used to say when I was a little dragon; but after all, that's a matter of opinion."

Gawaine was so helpless with terror that the dragon's confidence rose immeasurably and it could not resist the temptation to show off a bit.

"Could I possibly be of any assistance?" it asked. "What's the first letter of the magic word?"

"It begins with an 'r,'" said Gawaine weakly.

"Let's see," mused the dragon, "that doesn't tell us much, does it? What sort of a word is this? Is it an epithet, do you think?"

Gawaine could do no more than nod.

"Why, of course," exclaimed the dragon, "reactionary Republican."

Gawaine shook his head.

"Well, then," said the dragon, "we'd better get down to business. Will you surrender?"

With the suggestion of a compromise Gawaine mustered up enough courage to speak.

"What will you do if I surrender?" he asked.

"Why, I'll eat you," said the dragon.

"And if I don't surrender?"

"I'll eat you just the same."

"Then it doesn't mean any difference, does it?" moaned Gawaine.

"It does to me," said the dragon with a smile. "I'd rather you didn't surrender. You'd taste much better if you didn't."

The dragon waited for a long time for Gawaine to ask "Why?" but the boy was too frightened to speak. At last the dragon had to give the explanation without his cue line. "You see," he said, "if you don't surrender you'll taste better because you'll die game."

This was an old and ancient trick of the dragon's. By means of some such quip he was accustomed to paralyze his victims with laughter and then to destroy them. Gawaine was sufficiently paralyzed as it was, but laughter had no part in his helplessness. With the last word of the joke the dragon drew back his head and struck. In that second there flashed into the mind of Gawaine the magic word "Rumplesnitz," but there was no time to say it. There was time only to strike and, without a word,

Gawaine met the onrush of the dragon with a full swing. He put all his back and shoulders into it. The impact was terrific and the head of the dragon flew away almost a hundred yards and landed in a thicket.

Gawaine did not remain frightened very long after the death of the dragon. His mood was one of wonder. He was enormously puzzled. He cut off the ears of the monster almost in a trance. Again and again he thought to himself, "I didn't say 'Rumplesnitz'!" He was sure of that and yet there was no question that he had killed the dragon. In fact, he had never killed one so utterly. Never before had he driven a head for anything like the same distance. Twenty-five yards was perhaps his best previous record. All the way back to the knight school he kept rumbling about in his mind seeking an explanation for what had occurred. He went to the Headmaster immediately and after closing the door told him what had happened. "I didn't say 'Rumplesnitz,'" he explained with great earnestness.

The Headmaster laughed. "I'm glad you've found out," he said. "It makes you ever so much more of a hero. Don't you see that? Now you know that it was you who killed all these dragons and not that foolish little word 'Rumplesnitz.'"

Gawaine frowned. "Then it wasn't a magic word after all?" he asked.

"Of course not," said the Headmaster, "you ought to be too old for such foolishness. There isn't any such thing as a magic word."

"But you told me it was magic," protested Gawaine. "You said it was magic and now you say it isn't."

"It wasn't magic in a literal sense," answered the Headmaster, "but it was much more wonderful than that. The word gave you confidence. It took away your fears.

If I hadn't told you that you might have been killed the very first time. It was your battle-ax did the trick."

Gawaine surprised the Headmaster by his attitude. He was obviously distressed by the explanation. He interrupted a long philosophic and ethical discourse by the Headmaster with, "If I hadn't of hit 'em all mighty hard and fast any one of 'em might have crushed me like a, like a—" He fumbled for a word.

"Egg shell," suggested the Headmaster.

"Like an egg shell," assented Gawaine, and he said it many times. All through the evening meal people who sat near him heard him muttering, "Like an egg shell, like an egg shell."

The next day was clear, but Gawaine did not get up at dawn. Indeed, it was almost noon when the Headmaster found him cowering in bed, with the clothes pulled over his head. The principal called the Assistant Professor of Pleasaunce, and together they dragged the boy toward the forest.

"He'll be all right as soon as he gets a couple more dragons under his belt," explained the Headmaster.

"The Assistant Professor of Pleasaunce agreed. "It would be a shame to stop such a fine run," he said. "Why, counting that one yesterday, he's killed fifty dragons."

They pushed the boy into a thicket above which hung a meager cloud of steam. It was obviously quite a small dragon. But Gawaine did not come back that night or the next. In fact, he never came back. Some weeks afterward brave spirits from the school explored the thicket, but they could find nothing to remind them of Gawaine except the metal parts of his medals. Even the ribbons had been devoured.

The Headmaster and the Assistant Professor of Pleasaunce agreed that it would be just as well not to tell the school how Gawaine had achieved his record and still less how he came to die. They held that it might have a bad effect on school spirit. Accordingly, Gawaine has lived in the memory of the school as its greatest hero. No visitor succeeds in leaving the building to-day without seeing a great shield which hangs on the wall of the dining hall. Fifty pairs of dragons' ears are mounted upon the shield and underneath in gilt letters is "Gawaine le Cœur-Hardy," followed by the simple inscription, "He killed fifty dragons." The record has never been equaled.

The Race

When I got to the airport I rushed up to the desk
and they told me the flight was cancelled. The doctors had
said my father would not live through the night
and the flight was cancelled. A young man with a
dark blond moustache told me
another airline had a non-stop
leaving in seven minutes—see that
elevator over there well go
down to the first floor, make a right you'll
see a yellow bus, get off at the
second Pan Am terminal—I
ran, I who have no sense of direction
raced exactly where he'd told me, like a fish
slipping upstream deftly against the
flow of the river. I jumped off that bus with my
heavy bags and ran, the bags
wagged me from side to side as if to
prove I was under the claims of the material, I
ran up to a man with a white flower on his breast,
I who always go to the end of the line, I said
Help me. He looked at my ticket, he said make a
left and then a right go up the moving stairs and then
run. I raced up the moving stairs
two at a time, at the top I saw the
long hollow corridor and
then I took a deep breath. I said
goodbye to my body, goodbye to comfort, I
used my legs and heart as if I would
gladly use them up for this, to
touch him again in this life. I ran and the

big heavy dark bags
banged me, wheeled and swam around me like
planets in wild orbits—I have seen
pictures of women running down roads with their
belongings tied in black scarves
grasped in their fists, running under serious
gray historical skies—I blessed my
long legs he gave me, my strong
heart I abandoned to its own purpose, I
ran to Gate 17 and they were
just lifting the thick white
lozenge of the door to fit it into the
socket of the plane. Like the man who is not
too rich, I turned to the side and
slipped through the needle's eye, and then I
walked down the aisle toward my father. The jet was
full and people's hair was shining, they were
smiling, the interior of the plane was filled with a
mist of gold endorphin light.
I wept as people weep when they enter heaven,
in massive relief. We lifted up
gently from one tip of the continent and
did not stop until we set down lightly on the
other edge. I walked into his room and
watched his chest rise slowly and
sink again, all night
I watched him breathe.

SHARON OLDS

RIDE THE DARK HORSE

Margaret Bunel Edwards

Sometimes I wonder what I'm really like, inside. I feel as if I'm a mystery story, slowly revealing a plot to myself, but always in doubt as to what the outcome will be. I'd even reached a point where I figured it wasn't a bad idea to turn off. That way, I wouldn't have to face facts, wouldn't have to accept the consequences of what to do.

After all, if I didn't do anything, who would know whether I was broad-minded or prejudiced; a hero or a coward; capable or disorganized. Well, that's the way I used to think, until last summer. Then I found myself riding a dark horse and listening to a message, loud and clear, in that thundering water. Suddenly, I wanted to accept the challenge. Here's how it happened.

Right after breakfast, I left the Levesque Fishing Camp and headed along the narrow shoreline of the St. Maurice River toward Grandvue Rock. There I stood, my hands clenched deep in the pockets of my green nylon jacket, staring at the rapids, which only yesterday had dashed my hopes for a great holiday onto the rocks of my own carelessness.

I'd been coming to this camp with my dad for three years now, ever since I was thirteen. It's no secret that the river takes a mean turn at this bend, that the water plunges and rears over to shallows until a deeper channel gentles it down again and it flows on swiftly to Loretteville. I knew the danger, yet I drifted too close to the flecks of foam where an undercurrent swung the bow of my canoe against a jutting rock. The force tossed me, and some of the best fishing gear I'd ever worked for, into the water. Luckily, it's shallow there, but the pressure of the rushing water had my legs trembling and me gasping like a freshly hooked fish by the time I threw myself down onto the nice solid shore.

Disgusted, I glared at the channel ahead. To one side, an artificial sluiceway carried logs. To the other, the dark, racing water with its curling, swirling manes of white froth made me think of a herd of hard-sinewed horses. Well, when Dad got back from surveying timber farther upriver, he'd give me the horse laugh, all right. I must be the only dope around who'd forgotten that the dark water, even though it look wilder, is a better bet than the shallow, bubbling stretches that mask a treacherous riverbed.

When I heard footsteps sliding on the rocky path behind me, I straightened quickly, hoping that I looked merely nonchalant, instead of discouraged.

Jean Paul Levesque scrambled up beside me. He's big Joe's son and he's been my friend for the past three years. "*Bonjour, mon ami,*" he hailed me, his dark brown eyes sparkling. He was dressed as I was in blue jeans, but his shirt was a bright red plaid. "I have good news for you."

"Oh, sure, my fairy godmother waved her wand and

fixed my staved canoe," I commented sourly. "Then, using her magnetic personality, she dragged the rapids for my fishing gear."

"You *Anglais*," Jean Paul shrugged. "Why do you talk so fast that no one can understand, I do not make sense from your words. But *mon pere* say, if you like, you can have small job helping me to clear logs from the river. Soon you will earn enough to buy a new canoe, *n'est ce pas?*"

For the first time since my accident, I began to feel good. I turned away from the hypnotic, tumbling water and we started back to camp. The St. Maurice is used as a workhorse, when it comes to getting logs to the pulp mill at Loretteville. Though swift-flowing by nature, the left side is even faster because extra water is released into it from a dam. The logs literally race one another until they arrive, sleek and glistening, at the mill.

Sometimes the big tree trunks flip out of the sluiceway and then they float, half-submerged, a definite hazard to boats and canoes. These are the strays that a good worker, with a strong arm and a pike pole, can drag to the shore and reap a bounty from the mill owners. The pay's generous, so I figured it wouldn't take too long to make up my loss.

"Thanks, Jean Paul," I grinned. "Your dad's a great guy to offer me a job."

"The others around are all busy guiding the tourists," he explained. "So you and I have the river to ourselves."

We explored for awhile tracking back and forth, but never too far from the shoreline. The bush is dense and the going heavy, unless you can get into the open. Then we figured it might just be time for one of Madame Levesque's pancake lunches, complete with homemade maple syrup.

She is a plump, good-natured woman with big expressive eyes, which she uses to help her meagre knowledge of

English. She rolled them in concern when Jean Paul told her we were taking on the job of timber salvage. A regular barrage of French pinned him into his chair at the big kitchen table, where we were eating, but he just grinned and shrugged. "Mama sees a bear behind every tree," he explained, as we waved goodbye and headed for the wharf. "Between the bears and the river, we don't stand a chance."

"Aren't you forgetting the black flies," I asked, taking a swipe at a cloud of the pests, while we pushed off. "I guess that's what's meant when they say it's the *little* things in life that get to you."

By now, we were well into the current. My job was to sit in the bow, pike pole at the ready, and keep an eye on the swift sun-dappled water. The first log, although clearly visible, came at me so fast the canoe lifted dangerously. We rode up on the tree trunk but I managed to flail out, hook the bark and push with every ounce of my strength. My arms were aching by the time I'd brought our captive alongside. Jean Paul paddled expertly as we angled toward shore with the log in tow.

"*Bon,*" he shouted encouragingly. "By the end of the week, you'll be strong enough to crack a bear's ribs."

"If I'm able to stand up, you mean," I gasped, as we dragged the log clear of the water.

One hour and ten logs later, we were both ready for a short rest. I threw myself down on the narrow beach, thankful for the shade of the maples crowding the shoreline. Jean Paul reached into the canoe and took out his gear. I tried not to be envious at the sight of his fibreglass fishing pole, with its smooth-running reel. "There's a deeper spot back a little," he commented. "Think I'll do some casting."

I settled my head on my life jacket and closed my eyes. If those blasted flies would leave me in peace, I intended to rest up for the next bout with the river.

I must have dozed off because when my eyes snapped open, I was aware that the shadows had lengthened and that something had disturbed me. But what? Not one of Madame Levesque's bears, surely! Then the crashing, stumbling sound became clearer and I was on my feet instantly. "Jean Paul," I shouted and almost reeled back into the river as he came blundering into sight. He was falling, even as I reached him, and I could only help lower him to the ground.

My voice wouldn't work as I stared at him. His face, covered with blood, was pulled sideways and distended by a long, vicious sliver of glistening metal. His casting lure must have snagged a low branch and fallen back on him, I thought, feeling my stomach lurch at the sight of him. The hooks were embedded above his eye and through his cheek and seemed to be actually alive and evil, gleaming there in the sunlight. He'd torn his shirt in his wild dash and long cuts on his chest were wet and swelling. Already, a swarm of insidious black flies hovered over the open wounds.

I heard my cracked voice whispering in disbelief. "What will I do, what will I do," I kept saying, over and over, as I yanked on my life jacket and heaved at the canoe to ground it on the shore. The canoe had to be steadied before I could get him into it. I couldn't risk jarring those hooks, so close to his dazed eyes. While I made him as comfortable as possible on the bottom of the canoe, my mind was racing like the sluiceway.

Should I try to battle the current upriver, to the camp? But the men were in the bush and the thought of Madame's screeching at the sight of her son decided my course. I'd head for the doctor at Loretteville.

The shore flashed past as I paddled at top speed, glad of some physical action to counteract my mental turmoil. I was afraid of the rapids and there would not be any second chances today. I had to be ready to hit deep water as soon as we rounded the bend.

While I was still trying to get a grip on myself, I heard it. More than ever, the water's roar made me think of galloping horses and as the noise thudded against my eardrums and paced the straining tempo of my heartbeat, the two sounds seemed to merge into an inner rhythm that exhilarated, even as it terrified me.

Jean Paul half struggled to sit up, then collapsed back again. "You will *nevair* be able to make the portage with me," he whispered in despair.

"Portage?" I made it sound like a word they used on Mars—a word I'd never heard. "Keep low, *mon ami,* we're going to ride a dark horse."

And then I was breathing deeply in the spray-filled air, my paddle pressed hard back against the canoe to act as a rudder. Sweat oozed from my clenched hands as we darted between the rock walls, the water exploding over the shallow bed. The canoe trembled as she took the first shock of rushing water but I knew what I was looking for. We settled onto the nearest body, riding high beside the white foam mane. Once there, away from the pale slate water bubbling above the sharp stones, I held the paddle firm and guided the craft.

I suppose I breathed at least once before the bucking, straining horse finally slowed from his gallop to a canter and then, effortlessly slid us from his back. Personally, I was not conscious of using any part of me except my eyes. My hair hung down, soaked by the tossing stray, and I pushed it back as I swiped at my eyes with the back of my hand.

By now, although the going was easy, I felt exhausted; and when we finally glided to a smooth stop at the dock at Loretteville, I didn't have another ten metres left in me.

Work-roughened hands seemed to reach out from every direction to help me to my feet, to ease Jean Paul from the canoe. The air was thick with muttered curses as big, tough men tried to express their sympathy for Jean Paul. More than one huge arm flailed my back in a gesture of friendship and approval, and I wondered if I had escaped the rapids only to be pounded to pieces by my new friends.

A taxi was called to take us to the hospital and I was trying to think of enough French words to tell Madame Levesque on the telephone that there had been an accident, but everything was okay. I stared up the river for a long moment, warmed by the good feeling of having come through in the clutch.

Then it struck me. What if I hadn't given it a try? I'd never have known what I could do for a pal, when he so desperately needed my help.

I still feel like a mystery story inside. But now I'm not afraid to look over the clues to my personality; I'm not fearful of taking the action that will move the plot along. I know I'll find out that there will be times when I'm not a great guy; as well as times when I have what it takes.

At least I'll be doing, and living; and eventually, I may even understand myself.

THE STORY OF A
SHIPWRECKED
SAILOR

From the non-fiction book by
Gabriel García Márquez

THE GREAT NIGHT

The first thing I felt, plunged into darkness so thick I could no longer see the palm of my hand, was that I wouldn't be able to overcome the terror. From the slapping of the waves against the sides, I knew the raft was moving, slowly but inexorably. Sunk in darkness, I realized I hadn't felt so alone in the daytime. I was more alone in the dark, in a raft that I could no longer see but could feel beneath me, gliding silently over a dense sea filled with strange creatures. To make myself less lonely, I looked at the dial of my watch. It was ten minutes to seven. Much later—it seemed as if two or three hours had passed—it was five minutes to seven. When the minute hand reached twelve, it was exactly seven o'clock and the sky was packed with stars. But to me it seemed that so much time had passed, it should now be nearly dawn. Desperately I went on thinking about the planes.

I started to feel cold. In a life raft it's impossible to stay dry even for a minute. Even if you are seated on the gunwale, half your body is underwater because the bottom of the raft is shaped like a basket, extending more than half a meter below the surface. By eight o'clock the water was not as cold as the air. I knew that at the bottom of the raft I was safe from sea creatures because the rope mesh that protected the bottom prevented them from coming too close. But that's what you learn in school, and that's what you believe in school, when the instructor puts on a demonstration with a scale model of the life raft and you're seated on a bench among forty classmates at two o'clock in the afternoon. When you're alone at sea at eight o'clock at night, and without hope, the instructor's words make no sense at all. I knew that half of my body was in a realm that didn't belong to men but to the creatures of the sea, and that despite the icy wind whipping my shirt, I didn't dare move from the gunwale. According to the instructor, that was the least safe part of the raft. But all things considered, it was only there that I felt far enough away from the creatures: those immense unknown beasts I could hear passing the raft.

That night I had trouble finding Ursa Minor, lost in an endless maze of stars. I had never seen so many. It was hard to locate an empty space in the entire span of the sky. Once I spotted Ursa Minor, I didn't dare look anywhere else. I don't know why I felt less alone looking at Ursa Minor.

On shore leave in Cartagena, we often gathered at the Manga bridge in the small hours to listen to Ramón Herrera sing, imitating Daniel Santos while someone accompanied him on the guitar. Sitting on the wall of the stone bridge, I always found Ursa Minor on one side of the

Cerro de la Popa. That night, sitting on the gunwale of the raft, I felt for a moment as if I were back at the Manga bridge, with Ramón Herrera next to me singing to a guitar, and as if Ursa Minor weren't two hundred miles from Earth but, instead, up on top of the Cerro de la Popa itself. I imagined someone in Cartagena looking at Ursa Minor while I watched it from the sea, and that made me feel less lonely.

My first night at sea seemed very long because absolutely nothing happened. It is impossible to describe a night on a life raft, when nothing happens and you're scared of unseen creatures and you've got a watch with a glowing dial that you can't stop checking even for a minute. The night of February 28—my first night at sea—I looked at my watch every minute. It was torture. In desperation, I swore I would stop doing it and I'd stow the watch in my pocket, so as not to be so dependent on the time. I was able to resist until twenty to nine. I still wasn't hungry or thirsty, and I was sure I could hold out until the following day, when the planes would arrive. But I thought the watch would drive me crazy. A prisoner of anxiety, I took it off my wrist to stuff it in my pocket, but as I held it in my hand it occurred to me that it would be better to fling it into the sea. I hesitated a moment. Then I was terrified: I thought I would feel even more alone without the watch. I put it back on my wrist and began to look at it again, minute by minute, as I had in the afternoon when I searched the horizon for airplanes until my eyes began to hurt.

After midnight I wanted to cry. I hadn't slept for a moment, but I hadn't even wanted to. With the same hope I had felt in the afternoon as I waited for airplanes, that night I looked for the lights of ships. For hours I scrutinized the sea, a tranquil sea, immense and silent, but I didn't see a single light other than the stars.

The cold was more intense in the early hours of morning, and it seemed as if my body were glowing, with all the sun of the afternoon embedded under my skin. With the cold, it burned more intensely. From midnight on, my right knee began to hurt and I felt as though the water had penetrated to my bones. But these feelings were remote: I thought about my body less than about the lights of the ships. It seemed to me, in the midst of that infinite solitude, in the midst of the sea's dark murmur, that if I spotted the light of only a single ship, I would let out a yell that could be heard at any distance.

THE LIGHT OF EACH DAY

Dawn did not break slowly, as it does on land. The sky turned pale, the first stars disappeared, and I went on looking, first at my watch and then at the horizon. The contours of the sea began to appear. Twelve hours had passed, but it didn't seem possible. Night couldn't be as long as day. You have to have spent the night at sea, sitting in a life raft and looking at your watch, to know that the night is immeasurably longer than the day. But soon dawn begins to break, and then it's wearying to know it's another day.

That occurred to me on my first night in the raft. When dawn came, nothing else mattered. I thought neither of water nor of food. I didn't think of anything at all, until the wind turned warmer and the sea's surface grew smooth and golden. I hadn't slept a second all night, but at that moment it seemed as if I'd just awakened. When I stretched out in the raft my bones ached and my skin burned. But the day was brilliant and warm, and the murmur of the wind picking up gave me a new strength to continue waiting. And I felt profoundly composed in the life raft. For the first time in my twenty years of life, I was perfectly happy.

The raft continued to drift forward—how far it had gone during the night I couldn't calculate—but the horizon still looked exactly the same, as if I hadn't moved a centimeter. At seven o'clock I thought of the destroyer. It was breakfast time. I imagined my shipmates seated around the table eating apples. Then we would have eggs. Then meat. Then bread and coffee. My mouth filled with saliva and I could feel a slight twisting in my stomach. To take my mind off the idea of food, I submerged myself up to my neck in the bottom of the raft. The cool water on my sunburned back was soothing and made me feel stronger. I stayed submerged like that for a long time, asking myself why I had gone with Ramón Herrera to the stern deck instead of returning to my bunk to lie down. I reconstructed the tragedy minute by minute and decided I had been stupid. There was really no reason I should have been one of the victims: I wasn't on watch, I wasn't required on deck. When I concluded that everything that had happened was due to bad luck, I felt anxious again. But looking at my watch calmed me down. The day was moving along quickly: it was eleven-thirty.

A BLACK SPECK ON THE HORIZON

The approach of midday made me think about Cartagena again. I thought it was impossible they hadn't noticed I was missing. I began regretting that I had made it to the life raft; I imagined that my shipmates had been rescued and that I was the only one still adrift because my raft had been blown away by the wind. I even attributed reaching the life raft to bad luck.

That idea had hardly ripened when I thought I saw a speck on the horizon. I fixed my sights on the black point coming toward me. It was eleven-fifty. I watched so intently that the sky was soon filled with glittering points. But the black speck kept moving closer, heading directly toward the raft. Two minutes after I spotted it, I could make out its form perfectly. As it approached from the sky, luminous and blue, it threw off blinding, metallic flashes. Little by little I could distinguish it from the other bright specks. My neck started to hurt and my eyes could no longer tolerate the sky's brilliance. But I kept on looking: it was fast and gleaming, and it was coming directly toward the raft. At that moment I wasn't feeling happy. I felt no overwhelming emotion. I had a sense of great clarity and I felt extraordinarily calm as I stood in the raft while the plane approached. I took off my shirt slowly. I felt that I knew the exact moment when I should begin signaling with it. I stood there a minute, two minutes, with the shirt in my hand, waiting for the plane to come closer. It headed directly toward the raft. When I raised my arm and began to wave the shirt, I could hear, over the noise of the waves, the vibration of the plane's engines grow louder.

A Companion Aboard the Life Raft

For at least five minutes I waved my shirt furiously, but I quickly saw I had been mistaken: the plane wasn't coming toward the raft at all. As I watched the black speck growing larger, it seemed as if the plane would fly overhead. But it passed far away, too high to see me. Then it made a wide turn, started to head back, and disappeared into the sky from where it had appeared. Standing in the raft, exposed to the scorching sun, I looked at the black speck, not thinking about anything, as it erased itself completely from the horizon.

⤳

The waves crashed over the side. The raft danced on the turbulent sea, but I was secure, tied to the ropes by my belt. The oar was also secure. As I worked to ensure that the raft wouldn't overturn again, I realized I had nearly lost my shirt and shoes. If I hadn't been so cold, they would have been at the bottom of the raft, together with the other two oars, when it overturned.

It's perfectly normal for a raft to overturn in rough seas. The vessel is made of cork and covered with water-proof fabric painted white. But the bottom isn't rigid; it hangs from the cork frame like a basket. If the raft turns over in the water, the bottom immediately returns to its normal position. The only danger is in losing the raft. For that reason, I figured that as long as I was tied to it, the raft could turn over a thousand times without my losing it.

That was a fact. But there was one thing I hadn't foreseen. A quarter of an hour after the first one, the raft did a second spectacular somersault. First I was suspended in the icy, damp air, whipped by the gale. Then I saw hell right before my eyes: I realized which way the raft would turn over. I tried to move to the opposite side to provide equilibrium, but I was bound to the ropes by the thick leather belt. Instantly I realized what was happening: the raft had overturned completely. I was at the bottom, lashed firmly to the rope webbing. I was drowning; my hands searched frantically for the belt buckle to open it.

Panic-stricken but trying not to become confused, I thought how to undo the buckle. I knew I hadn't wasted much time: in good physical condition I could stay underwater more than eighty seconds. As soon as I had found myself under the raft, I had stopped breathing. That was at least five seconds gone. I ran my hand around my waist and in less than a second, I think, I found the belt. In another second I found the buckle. It was fastened to the ropes in such a way that I had to push myself away from the raft with my other hand to release it. I wasted time looking for a place to grab hold. Then I pushed off with my left hand. My right hand grasped the buckle, oriented itself quickly, and loosened the belt. Keeping the buckle open, I lowered my body toward the bottom, without letting go of the side, and in a fraction of a second I was free of the ropes. I felt my lungs gasping for breath. With one last effort, I grabbed the side with both hands and pulled with all my strength, still not breathing. Bringing my full weight to bear on it, I succeeded in turning the raft over again. But I was still underneath it.

I was swallowing water. My throat, ravaged by thirst, burned terribly. But I barely noticed. The important thing was not to let go of the raft. I managed to raise my head to the surface. I breathed. I was so tired. I didn't think I had the strength to lift myself over the side. But I was terrified to be in the same water that had been infested with sharks only hours before. Absolutely certain it would be the final effort of my life, I called on my last reserves of energy, leaped over the side, and fell exhausted into the bottom of the raft.

I don't know how long I lay there, face up, with my throat burning and my raw fingertips throbbing. But I do know I was concerned with only two things: that my lungs quiet down and that the raft not turn over again.

The Sun at Daybreak

That was how my eighth day at sea dawned. The morning was stormy. If it had rained, I wouldn't have had the strength to collect drinking water. I thought rain would revive me, but not a drop fell, even though the humidity in the air was like an announcement of imminent rain. The sea was still choppy at daybreak. It didn't calm down until after eight, but then the sun came out and the sky turned an intense blue again.

Completely spent, I lay down at the side of the raft and took a few swallows of sea water. I now know that it's not harmful to the body. But I didn't know it then, and I only resorted to it when the pain in my throat became unbearable. After seven days at sea, thirst is a feeling unto itself; it's a deep pain in the throat, in the sternum, and especially beneath the clavicles. And it's also the fear of suffocating. The sea water relieved the pain.

After a storm the sea turns blue, as in pictures. Near the shore, tree trunks and roots torn up by the storm float gently along. Gulls emerge to fly over the water. That morning, when the breeze died down, the surface of the water turned metallic and the raft glided along in a straight line. The warm wind felt reassuring to my body and my spirit.

A big old dark gull flew over the raft. I had no doubt then that I was near land. The sea gull I had captured a few days earlier was a young bird. At that age they can fly great distances—they can be found many miles into the interior. But an old sea gull, big and heavy like the one I had just seen couldn't fly a hundred miles from shore. I felt renewed strength. As I had done on the first days, I began to search the horizon again. Vast numbers of sea gulls came from every direction.

I had company and I was happy. I wasn't hungry. More and more frequently I took drinks of sea water. I wasn't lonely in the midst of the immense number of sea gulls circling over my head. I remembered Mary Address.

What had become of her? I wondered, remembering her voice when she translated the dialogue for me at the movies. In fact, on that day—the only one on which I had thought of Mary Address for no reason at all, and surely not because the sky was full of sea gulls—Mary was at a Catholic church in Mobile hearing a mass for the eternal rest of my soul. That mass, as Mary later wrote to me in Cartagena, was celebrated on the eighth day of my disappearance. It was for the repose of my soul, but I now think it was also for the repose of my body, for that morning, while I thought about Mary Address and she attended mass in Mobile, I was happy at sea, watching the sea gulls that proved land was near.

I spent almost all day sitting on the side of the raft, searching the horizon. The day was startlingly clear, and I was certain I saw land once from a distance of fifty miles. The raft had assumed a speed that two men with oars couldn't have equaled. It moved in a straight line, as if propelled by a motor along the calm, blue surface.

After spending seven days on a raft one can detect the slightest change in the color of the water. On March 7, at three-thirty in the afternoon, I noticed that the raft had reached an area where the water wasn't blue, but dark green. There was a definite demarcation: on one side was the blue water I had been seeing for seven days; on the other, green water that looked denser. The sky was full of sea gulls flying very low. I could hear them flapping over my head. The signs were unmistakable: the change in the color of the water and the abundance of sea gulls told me I should keep a vigil that night, alert for the first lights of shore.

Ayii, Ayii,
I think over again my small adventures
When with the wind I drifted in my kayak
And thought I was in danger.
My fears,
Those small ones that seemed so big,
For all the vital things
I had to get and to reach.
And yet there is only one great thing,
The only thing,
To live to see the great day that dawns
And the light that fills the world.

EASTERN INUIT

The Power of Light

A non-fiction story from the
book *Stories for Children*
by Isaac Bashevis Singer

During World War II, after the Nazis had bombed and bombed the Warsaw ghetto, a boy and a girl were hiding in one of the ruins—David, fourteen years old, and Rebecca, sixteen.

It was winter and bitter cold outside. For weeks Rebecca had not left the dark, partially collapsed cellar that was their hiding place, but every few days David would go out to search for food. All the stores had been destroyed in the bombing, and David sometimes found stale bread, cans of food, or whatever else had been buried. Making his way through the ruins was dangerous. Sometimes bricks and mortar would fall down, and he could easily lose his way. But if he and Rebecca did not want to die from hunger, he had to take the risk.

That day was one of the coldest. Rebecca sat on the ground wrapped in all the garments she possessed; still, she could not get warm. David had left many hours before, and Rebecca listened in the darkness for the sound of his return, knowing that if he did not come back nothing remained to her but death.

Suddenly she heard heavy breathing and the sound of a bundle being dropped. David had made his way home. Rebecca could not help but cry "David!"

"Rebecca!"

In the darkness they embraced and kissed. Then David said, "Rebecca, I found a treasure."

"What kind of treasure?"

"Cheese, potatoes, dried mushrooms, and a package of candy—and I have another surprise for you."

"What surprise?"

"Later."

Both were too hungry for a long talk. Ravenously they ate the frozen potatoes, the mushrooms, and part of the cheese. They each had one piece of candy. Then Rebecca asked, "What is it now, day or night?"

"I think night has fallen," David replied. He had a wristwatch and kept track of day and night and also of the days of the week and the month. After a while Rebecca asked again, "What is the surprise?"

"Rebecca, today is the first day of Hanukkah, and I found a candle and some matches."

"Hanukkah tonight?"

"Yes."

"Oh, my!"

"I am going to bless the Hanukkah candle," David said.

He lit a match and there was light. Rebecca and David stared at their hiding place—bricks, pipes, and the uneven ground. He lighted the candle. Rebecca blinked her eyes. For the first time in weeks she really saw David. His hair was matted and his face streaked with dirt, but his eyes shone with joy. In spite of the starvation and persecution

David had grown taller, and he seemed older than his age and manly. Young as they both were, they had decided to marry if they could manage to escape from war-ridden Warsaw. As a token of their engagement, David had given Rebecca a shiny groschen he found in his pocket on the day when the building where both of them lived was bombed.

Now David pronounced the benediction over the Hanukkah candle, and Rebecca said, "Amen." They had both lost their families, and they had good reason to be angry with God for sending them so many afflictions, but the light of the candle brought peace into their souls. That glimmer of light, surrounded by so many shadows, seemed to say without words: Evil has not yet taken complete dominion. A spark of hope is still left.

For some time David and Rebecca had thought about escaping from Warsaw. But how? The ghetto was watched by the Nazis day and night. Each step was dangerous. Rebecca kept delaying their departure. It would be easier in the summer, she often said, but David knew that in their predicament they had little chance of lasting until then. Somewhere in the forest there were young men and women called partisans who fought the Nazi invaders. David wanted to reach them. Now, by the light of the Hanukkah candle, Rebecca suddenly felt renewed courage. She said, "David, let's leave."

"When?"

"When you think it's the right time," she answered.

"The right time is now," David said. "I have a plan."

For a long time David explained the details of his plan to Rebecca. It was more than risky. The Nazis had enclosed the ghetto with barbed wire and posted guards armed with machine guns on the surrounding roofs. At night searchlights lit up all possible exits from the destroyed ghetto. But in his wanderings through the ruins,

David had found an opening to a sewer which he thought might lead to the other side. David told Rebecca that their chances of remaining alive were slim. They could drown in the dirty water or freeze to death. Also, the sewers were full of hungry rats. But Rebecca agreed to take the risk; to remain in the cellar for the winter would mean certain death.

When the Hanukkah light began to sputter and flicker before going out, David and Rebecca gathered their few belongings. She packed the remaining food in a kerchief, and David took his matches and a piece of lead pipe for a weapon.

. . . David and Rebecca were soon on their way through the ruins. They came to passages so narrow they had to crawl on hands and knees. But the food they had eaten, and the joy the Hanukkah candle had awakened in them, gave them the courage to continue. After some time David found the entrance to the sewer. Luckily the sewage had frozen, and it seemed that the rats had left because of the extreme cold. From time to time David and Rebecca stopped to rest and to listen. After a while they crawled on, slowly and carefully. Suddenly they stopped in their tracks. From above they could hear the clanging of a trolley car. They had reached the other side of the ghetto. All they needed now was to find a way to get out of the sewer and to leave the city as quickly as possible.

Many miracles seemed to happen that Hanukkah night. Because the Nazis were afraid of enemy planes, they had ordered a complete blackout. Because of the bitter cold, there were fewer Gestapo guards. David and Rebecca managed to leave the sewer and steal out of the city without being caught. At dawn they reached a forest where they were able to rest and have a bite to eat.

Even though the partisans were not very far from Warsaw, it took David and Rebecca a week to reach them.

They walked at night and hid during the days—sometimes in granaries and sometimes in barns. Some peasants stealthily helped the partisans and those who were running away from the Nazis. From time to time David and Rebecca got a piece of bread, a few potatoes, a radish, or whatever the peasants could spare. In one village they encountered a Jewish partisan who had come to get food for his group. He belonged to the Haganah, an organization that sent men from Israel to rescue Jewish refugees from the Nazis in occupied Poland. This young man brought David and Rebecca to the other partisans who roamed the forest. It was the last day of Hanukkah, and that evening the partisans lit eight candles. Some of them played dreidel on the stump of an oak tree while others kept watch.

From the day David and Rebecca met the partisans, their life became like a tale in a storybook. They joined more and more refugees who all had but one desire—to settle in the Land of Israel. They did not always travel by train or bus. They walked. They slept in stables, in burned-out houses, and wherever they could hide from the enemy. To reach their destination, they had to cross Czechoslovakia, Hungary, and Yugoslavia. Somewhere at the seashore in Yugoslavia, in the middle of the night, a small boat manned by a Haganah crew waited for them, and all the refugees with their meagre belongings were packed into it. This all happened silently and in great secrecy, because the Nazis occupied Yugoslavia.

But their dangers were far from over. Even though it was spring, the sea was stormy and the boat was too small for such a long trip. Nazi planes spied the boat and tried without success to sink it with bombs. They also feared the Nazi submarines which were lurking in the depths. There was nothing the refugees could do besides pray to

God, and this time God seemed to hear their prayers, because they managed to land safely.

The Jews of Israel greeted them with a love that made them forget their suffering. They were the first refugees who had reached the Holy Land, and they were offered all the help and comfort that could be given. Rebecca and David found relatives in Israel who accepted them with open arms, and although they had become quite emaciated, they were basically healthy and recovered quickly. After some rest they were sent to a special school where foreigners were taught modern Hebrew. Both David and Rebecca were diligent students. After finishing high school, David was able to enter the academy of engineering in Haifa, and Rebecca, who excelled in languages and literature, studied in Tel Aviv—but they always met on weekends. When Rebecca was eighteen, she and David were married. They found a small house with a garden in Ramat Gan, a suburb of Tel Aviv.

I know all this because David and Rebecca told me their story on a Hanukkah evening in their house in Ramat Gan about eight years later. The Hanukkah candles were burning, and Rebecca was frying potato pancakes served with applesauce for all of us. David and I were playing dreidel with their little son, Menahem Eliezer, named after both of his grandfathers. David told me that this large wooden dreidel was the same one the partisans had played with on that Hanukkah evening in the forest in Poland. Rebecca said to me, "If it had not been for that little candle David brought to our hiding place, we wouldn't be sitting here today. That glimmer of light awakened in us a hope and strength we didn't know we possessed. We'll give the dreidel to Menahem Eliezer when he is old enough to understand what we went through and how miraculously we were saved."

From the autobiography
West with the Night
by Beryl Markham

"If you are still determined to fly the Atlantic this late in the year," the voice said, "the Air Ministry suggests that the weather it is able to forecast for tonight, and for tomorrow morning, will be about the best you can expect."

The voice had a few other things to say, but not many, and then it was gone, and I lay in bed half-suspecting that the telephone call and the man who made it were only parts of the mediocre dream I had been dreaming. I felt that if I closed my eyes the unreal quality of the message would be re-established, and that, when I opened them again, this would be another ordinary day with its usual beginning and its usual routine.

But of course I could not close my eyes, nor my mind, nor my memory. I could lie there for a few moments— remembering how it had begun, and telling myself, with senseless repetition, that by tomorrow morning I should either have flown the Atlantic to America—or I should not have flown it. In either case this was the day I would try.

"... J.C., why don't you finance Beryl for a record flight?"

I could lie there staring lazily at the ceiling and recall J.C.'s dry answer: "A number of pilots have flown the North Atlantic, west to east. Only Jim Mollison has done it alone the other way—from Ireland. Nobody has done it alone from England—man or woman. I'd be interested in that, but nothing else. If you want to try it, Burl, I'll back you. I think Edgar Percival could build a plane that would do it, provided you can fly it. Want to chance it?"

"Yes."

I could remember saying that better than I could remember anything—except J.C.'s almost ghoulish grin, and his remark that sealed the agreement: "It's a deal, Burl. I'll furnish the plane and you fly the Atlantic—but, gee, I wouldn't tackle it for a million. Think of all that black water! Think how cold it is!"

And I had thought of both.

I had thought of both for a while, and then there had been other things to think about. I had moved to Elstree, a half-hour's flight from the Percival Aircraft Works at Gravesend, and almost daily for three months now I had flown down to the factory in a hired plane and watched the Vega Gull they were making for me. I had watched her birth and watched her growth. I had watched her wings take shape, and seen wood and fabric moulded to her ribs to form her long, sleek belly, and I had seen her engine cradled into her frame, and made fast.

The Gull had a turquoise-blue body and silver wings. Edgar Percival had made her with care, with skill, and with worry — the care of a veteran flyer, the skill of a master designer, and the worry of a friend. Actually the plane was a standard sport model with a range of only six hundred and sixty miles. But she had a special under-carriage built to carry the weight of her extra oil and petrol tanks. The tanks were fixed into the wings, into the centre section, and into the cabin itself. In the cabin they formed a wall around my seat, and each tank had a pet-cock of its own. The petcocks were important.

"If you open one," said Percival, "without shutting the other first, you may get an airlock. You know the tanks in the cabin have no gauges, so it may be best to let one run completely dry before opening the next. Your motor might go dead in the interval—but she'll start again. She's a De Havilland Gipsy—and Gipsys never stop."

I had talked to Tom. We had spent hours going over the Atlantic chart, and I had realized that the tinker of Mole, now one of England's great pilots, had traded his dreams and had got in return a better thing. Tom had grown older too; he had jettisoned a deadweight of irrele-vant hopes and wonders, and had left himself a realistic code that had no room for temporizing or easy sentiment.

"I'm glad you're going to do it, Beryl. It won't be sim-ple. If you can get off the ground in the first place, with such an immense load of fuel, you'll be alone in that plane about a night and a day—mostly night. Doing it east to west, the wind's against you. In September, so is the weather. You won't have a radio. If you misjudge your course only a few degrees, you'll end up in Labrador or in the sea—so don't misjudge anything."

Tom could still grin. He had grinned; he had said: "Anyway, it ought to amuse you to think that your finan-cial backer lives on a farm called 'Place of Death' and your plane is being built at 'Gravesend.' If you were consistent, you'd christen the Gull 'The Flying Tombstone.'"

I hadn't been that consistent. I had watched the build-ing of the plane and I had trained for the flight like an athlete. And now, as I lay in bed, fully awake, I could still hear the quiet voice of the man from the Air Ministry intoning, like the voice of a dispassionate court clerk: ". . . the weather for tonight and tomorrow . . . will be about the best you can expect." I should have liked to discuss the flight once more with Tom before I took off, but he was on a special job up north. I got out of bed and bathed and put on my flying clothes and took some cold chicken packed in a cardboard box and flew over to the military field at Abingdon, where the Vega Gull waited for me under the care of the R.A.F. I remember that the weather was clear and still. . . .

So there behind me is Cork; and ahead of me is Berehaven Lighthouse. It is the last light, standing on the last land. I watch it, counting the frequency of its flashes—so many to the minute. Then I pass it and fly out to sea.

The fear is gone now—not overcome nor reasoned away. It is gone because something else has taken its place; the confidence and the trust, the inherent belief in the security of land underfoot—now this faith is transferred to my plane, because the land has vanished and there is no other tangible thing to fix faith upon. Flight is but momentary escape from the eternal custody of earth.

Rain continues to fall, and outside the cabin it is totally dark. My altimeter says that the Atlantic is two thousand feet below me, my Sperry Artificial Horizon says that I am flying level. I judge my drift at three degrees more than my weather chart suggests, and fly accordingly. I am flying blind. A beam to follow would help. So would a radio—but then, so would clear weather. The voice of the man at the Air Ministry had not promised storm.

I feel the wind rising and the rain falls hard. The smell of petrol in the cabin is so strong and the roar of the plane so loud that my senses are almost deadened. Gradually it becomes unthinkable that existence was ever otherwise.

At ten o'clock P.M. I am flying along the Great Circle Course for Harbour Grace, Newfoundland, into a forty-mile headwind at a speed of one hundred and thirty miles an hour. Because of the weather, I cannot be sure of how many more hours I have to fly, but I think it must be between sixteen and eighteen.

At ten-thirty I am still flying on the large cabin tank of petrol, hoping to use it up and put an end to the liquid swirl that has rocked the plane since my take-off. The tank has no gauge, but written on its side is the assurance: "This tank is good for four hours."

There is nothing ambiguous about such a guaranty. I believe it, but at twenty-five minutes to eleven, my motor coughs and dies, and the Gull is powerless above the sea.

I realize that the heavy drone of the plane has been, until this moment, complete and comforting silence. It is the actual silence following the last splutter of the engine that stuns me. I can't feel any fear; I can't feel anything. I can only observe with a kind of stupid disinterest that my hands are violently active and know that, while they move, I am being hypnotized by the needle of my altimeter.

I suppose that the denial of natural impulse is what is meant by "keeping calm," but impulse has reason in it. If it is night and you are sitting in an airplane with a stalled motor, and there are two thousand feet between you and the sea, nothing can be more reasonable than the impulse to pull back your stick in the hope of adding to that two thousand, if only by a little. The thought, the knowledge, the law that tells you that your hope lies not in this, but in a contrary act—the act of directing your impotent craft toward the water—seems a terrifying abandonment, not only of reason, but of sanity. Your mind and your heart reject it. It is your hands—your stranger's hands—that follow with unfeeling precision the letter of the law.

I sit there and watch my hands push forward on the stick and feel the Gull respond and begin its dive to the sea. Of course it is a simple thing; surely the cabin tank has run dry too soon. I need only to turn another petcock . . .

But it is dark in the cabin. It is easy to see the luminous dial of the altimeter and to note that my height is now eleven hundred feet, but it is not easy to see a petcock that is somewhere near the floor of the plane. A hand gropes and reappears with an electric torch, and fingers, moving with agonizing composure, find the petcock and turn it; and I wait.

At three hundred feet the motor is still dead, and I am conscious that the needle of my altimeter seems to whirl like the spoke of a spindle winding up the remaining distance between the plane and the water. There is some lightning, but the quick flash only serves to emphasize the darkness. How high can waves reach—twenty feet, perhaps? Thirty?

It is impossible to avoid the thought that this is the end of my flight, but my reactions are not orthodox; the various incidents of my entire life do not run through my mind like a motion-picture film gone mad. I only feel that all this has happened before—and it has. It has all happened a hundred times in my mind, in my sleep, so that now I am not really caught in terror; I recognize a familiar scene, a familiar story with its climax dulled by too much telling.

I do not know how close to the waves I am when the motor explodes to life again. But the sound is almost meaningless. I see my hand easing back on the stick, and I feel the Gull climb up into the storm, and I see the altimeter whirl like a spindle again, paying out the distance between myself and the sea.

The storm is strong. It is comforting. It is like a friend shaking me and saying, "Wake up! You were only dreaming."

But soon I am thinking. By simple calculation I find that my motor had been silent for perhaps an instant more than thirty seconds.

I ought to thank God—and I do, though indirectly. I thank Geoffrey De Havilland who designed the indomitable Gipsy, and who, after all, must have been designed by God in the first place. . . .

Success breeds confidence. But who has a right to confidence except the Gods? I had a following wind, my last tank of petrol was more than three-quarters full, and the world was as bright to me as if it were a new world, never touched. If I had been wiser, I might have known that such moments are, like innocence, short-lived. My engine began to shudder before I saw the land. It died, it spluttered, it started again and limped along. It coughed and spat black exhaust toward the sea.

There are words for everything. There was a word for this—airlock, I thought. This had to be an airlock because there was petrol enough. I thought I might clear it by turning on and turning off all the empty tanks, and so I did that. The handles of the petcocks were sharp little pins of metal, and when I had opened and closed them a dozen times, I saw that my hands were bleeding and that the blood was dropping on my maps and on my clothes, but the effort wasn't any good. I coasted along on a sick and halting engine. The oil pressure and the oil temperature gauges were normal, the magnetos working, and yet I lost altitude slowly while the realization of failure seeped into my heart. If I made the land, I should have been the first to fly the North Atlantic from England, but from my point of view, from a pilot's point of view, a forced landing was failure because New York was my goal. If only I could land and then take off, I would make it still . . . if only, if only . . .

The engine cuts again, and then catches, and each time it spurts to life I climb as high as I can get, and then it splutters and stops and I glide once more toward the water, to rise again and descend again, like a hunting sea bird.

I find the land. Visibility is perfect now and I see land forty or fifty miles ahead. If I am on my course, that will be Cape Breton. Minute after minute goes by. The minutes almost materialize; they pass before my eyes like links in a long slow-moving chain, and each time the engine cuts, I see a broken link in the chain and catch my breath until it passes.

The land is under me. I snatch my map and stare at it to confirm my whereabouts. I am, even at my present crippled speed, only twelve minutes from Sydney Airport, where I can land for repairs and then go on.

The engine cuts once more and I begin to glide, but now I am not worried; she will start again, as she has done, and I will gain altitude and fly into Sydney.

But she doesn't start. This time she's dead as death; the Gull settles earthward and it isn't any earth I know. It is black earth stuck with boulders and I hang above it, on hope and on a motionless propeller. Only I cannot hang above it long. The earth hurries to meet me, I bank, turn, and sideslip to dodge the boulders, my wheels touch, and I feel them submerge. The nose of the plane is engulfed in mud, and I go forward striking my head on the glass of the cabin front, hearing it shatter, feeling blood pour over my face.

I stumble out of the plane and sink to my knees in muck and stand there foolishly staring, not at the lifeless land, but at my watch.

Twenty-one hours and twenty-five minutes.

Atlantic flight. Abingdon, England, to a nameless swamp—nonstop.

A Cape Breton Islander found me—a fisherman trudging over the bog saw the Gull with her tail in the air and her nose buried, and then he saw me floundering in the embracing soil of his native land. I had been wandering for an hour and the black mud had got up to my waist and the blood from the cut in my head had met the mud halfway.

From a distance, the fisherman directed me with his arms and with shouts toward the firm places in the bog, and for another hour I walked on them and came toward him like a citizen of Hades blinded by the sun, but it wasn't the sun; I hadn't slept for forty hours.

He took me to his hut on the edge of the coast and I found that built upon the rocks there was a little cubicle that housed an ancient telephone—put there in case of shipwrecks.

I telephoned to Sydney Airport to say that I was safe and to prevent a needless search being made. On the following morning I did step out of a plane at Floyd Bennett Field and there was a crowd of people still waiting there to greet me, but the plane I stepped from was not the Gull, and for days while I was in New York I kept thinking about that and wishing over and over again that it had been the Gull, until the wish lost its significance, and time moved on, overcoming many things it met on the way.

George Gray

I have studied many times
The marble which was chiseled for me—
A boat with a furled sail at rest in a harbor.
In truth it pictures not my destination
But my life.
For love was offered me and I shrank from its disillusionment;
Sorrow knocked at my door, but I was afraid;
Ambition called to me, but I dreaded the chances.
Yet all the while I hungered for meaning in my life.
And now I know that we must lift the sail
And catch the winds of destiny
Wherever they drive the boat.
To put meaning in one's life may end in madness.
But life without meaning is the torture
Of restlessness and vague desire—
It is a boat longing for the sea and yet afraid.

EDGAR LEE MASTERS

GUM LIN
and
LOY YI LUNG

A Chinese myth
retold by Merlin Stone

Young and old, the women gather and walk slowly to the foot of Tai Ma Shan—Great Horse Mountain. There they stand side by side in the light of the waning moon, the third moon of the new year, and by the flowing waters of the river that wash the foot of the mountain, the riverbank lit by the twenty-one day old moon, they send their voices across the waters. Soft and loud, high and deep, the voices float off together into the night air— carrying with them the most wondrous of tales, the story of Loy Yi Lung, the dragon's daughter, and of the girl who had once lived in their village in times long ago, the brave and loving Gum Lin—Golden Lotus.

At first there is a sadness in the voices of the women, as they sing of the time of the dryness of the land, when the water was so scarce that the rice would not grow, when the bamboo withered and died in the drying mud of the gullies that had once been the beds of flowing streams. They sing of Gum Lin, when she was not yet a woman, and how she had gone about her work, her small hands cutting the reeds, her small fingers tying them together, making bamboo brooms, making bamboo mats—and selling all that she had made to help to feed her family.

As the land grew dryer and more barren, further and further from home did Gum Lin have to wander, searching for a few stalks of bamboo, when all that had grown close to the village had been stricken by the thirst of their roots. Miles from home she walked, into the deep forest thick with trees, making her own path between the great rocks, until far beyond the tall trees, at the foothills of the mountains, she saw what seemed to be an image in a dream. Thickets of bamboo, tall and yellow green, bent gently in the soft wind, clustering along the edges of a clear blue lake, a secret bowl of water in the mountains, one that she had never seen before. Gathering all that she could carry, Gum Lin returned to her village with her precious bamboo treasure.

All through the long night she tossed upon her sleeping mat. So much water in the forest where few can drink. So little water in the village where thirst was part of every day. The slender reeds of dream wove in and out through her restless sleep, until they wove themselves into a channel, a canal that the water could pour through—a canal in which the waters of the forest lake could find their way into the thirsty village, there filling up the muddy ditches where other waters had once run.

In the light of the early morning, a shovel and a pickaxe balanced upon her small shoulder, her long black hair braided tightly to last the rigours of the hard day's work ahead, Gum Lin started on the way that led to the clear blue mountain lake. There she planned to dig a pitcher spout on the rim of the reservoir of water, so that it would pour from the foothills of the mountain, into the thirsty gullies of the village from which the rice and bamboo had once been free to drink their fill. But arriving at the water's edge, she noticed a thick grove of trees on one side, and rocky ledges and boulders along another. By the rim of the great cup that held the deep, gathered, mountain waters, Gum Lin walked and looked, hoping to find the right place—until, just a few steps before her, in a place where she had thought she might dig, she saw a great stone gate.

She pulled upon the door of the gate, but it would not open. She picked and pried with the tip of her axe, but the door was very thick and tightly bolted. Stopping for a moment to catch her breath and to think of what to do, Gum Lin was surprised by a strange voice, and turning to see from where it came, all she could see was a wild grey swan that had made its way almost to where she stood at the edge of the lake. Again she heard the voice. Could it be the red ringed throat of the swan that was saying, "These waters are yours, once you find the key to the stone gate." There was no one else in sight, but by the time she thought to ask the wild swan if it had been speaking, and if so, where this special key might be found—the graceful wild bird had already made its way far across the wide lake.

Needing time to solve the puzzle, Gum Lin wandered back into the forest, winding her way between the cypress trees, thinking about the strange gate, wondering about the key to its latch. She had hardly noticed the three brightly feathered birds perched up high on the branch of a gnarled cypress, until voices, that seemed to come from where they sat, sang out in perfect chorus, "The daughter of the dragon. The daughter of the dragon." But just as

Gum Lin was about to ask the birds if they had truly spoken, three pairs of wings of brilliant colour slid into the air, waving as if in farewell. Gum Lin would have been more puzzled yet, had she not taken notice of the tail of a peacock, as it spread out against a tall pine, fanned open as wide as it could be. Suddenly the peacock shook its tail into a blur of blues and greens, and in the sound of the rustle of the feathers, Gum Lin heard these words, "Go to the edge of Ye Tiyoh, Wild Swan Lake. Stand upon its banks and sing the songs of your people. Make your voice loud and clear, so that the daughter of the dragon may hear you, and if your songs please her, she will come to you." And then the peacock folded its fan of eyes into a long tail, that followed behind its soft round body, and walked further into the dark woods.

The small legs of Gum Lin, still carrying the weight of pick and shovel, moved as fast as they could, back to the water's edge. Standing her tools beside her in the dirt, she leaned upon the handles, breathed deeply in, and then chanted out in a voice that was as clear as the blue lake water. She sang songs of the snow on the mountains, of the peaks that one could see from the village, of grass as green as that which she had been told once grew, of the loveliness of flowers that she had never seen—but though she sang song after song—nothing happened. The daughter of the dragon had chosen not to listen.

Determined to follow the peacock's instructions, Gum Lin thought of every song she knew. When she had finished the songs of the loveliness of nature, she began to sing the songs of the people of her village, of those who worked in the flooded fields of rice, of those who could not work now that they were dry. She sang the songs the women sang, as they wove the reeds, or as they repaired family huts after strong winds had blown them apart, or as they tried to feed the small but hungry mouths of new existence. They were proud songs, of people who did the best they could, but they were not the pretty songs of grass and flowers and snow capped mountains. Surely if the other songs had not brought the dragon's daughter forth, these songs would please her even less. Still Gum Lin sang.

Singing of the hardships of her people, of the loving kindness that they gave to one another, when there was little else to give, tears came to the dark brown eyes of Gum Lin, blurring her vision of Loy Yi Lung, the daughter of the dragon—as she emerged from the waters of the lake. Wiping the tears from her cheeks, Gum Lin soon remembered why she had been singing and called out to the daughter of the dragon, "The key. Please may I have the key? My people are dying of hunger. They work very hard but without water they have no food, without water the rice cannot grow."

"The key is in my father's cave on the deepest floor of the lake," Loy Yi Lung answered. "There he guards it, as he jealously guards all his worldly treasures—and would destroy anyone who might dare to intrude—even his own daughter." Then growing from a moment of further thought, a scheme was devised by the daughter of the dragon, who knew the dragon as well as he could be known. "Often when I sing just outside the cave, my father crawls closer to the entrance to listen to my song. Perhaps if we sang together, our voices would bring him to the entrance, and while I continued to sing, you could slip past him and search for the key."

All proceeded just as the two had planned, but when the brave young Gum Lin found herself in the darkness of the cave, she was overwhelmed by the sight of trunks and vessels piled high with golden coins and precious gems.

For a moment she thought to stuff her pockets with the jewels and gold, for with them she could move her family to better land, but then remembering the others of the village, the hungry crying infants, the weakened grandparents, those who still searched daily for any rice plant that might have survived the drought, she knew that she could not leave the cavern until she had found the key to the waters. Just at that moment, the edge of her shoulder upset a small ivory box that sat upon a rocky ledge. As it fell, it tumbled its contents out upon the watery stone floor—and there before her lay the key, golden and glowing, a carefully formed swan at its top, swimming in a sea of pearls that had long nestled against it in the box.

The key safely tucked inside her pocket, Gum Lin swam quietly past the dragon's side, and reaching the place where Loy Yi Lung still sang, she grasped her hand in joyous triumph. Side by side they swam to the edge of the mountain lake, to the place where the stone gate stood. Loy Yi Lung watched from the water, as Gum Lin climbed back upon the bank, and slipped the key into the long unused lock, turning it this way and that, pulling upon the handle of the door with all the strength of her small arms—until suddenly the door flew open as if being pushed from the other side! It was in this way that the water that had pressed upon the door rushed forth upon the grassy lakeside, digging deep into the ground—carving its own canal.

The water swam until it reached the dry waiting stream bed of the village. It sped along, diving over rocks, thinking only to quench the thirst of the ground where the rice and bamboo had once grown. It danced joyfully about the ankles of the few remaining plants, and tenderly bathed the seeds and ailing saplings, tucking them in their moist bed to rest, humming lullabies of how tall they would grow as it bubbled by. It tunnelled beneath the earth to leap inside the stone walls of wells, pouring itself into the cups of the thirsty. Ye Tiyoh Lake had stretched out its merciful river arm, spread its blue palms and fingers open in offering, to share itself with the people in the village of Tai Ma Shan.

Gum Lin walked along the river banks, following the path that the water had chosen into the village, as Loy Yi Lung swam alongside, relieved that the angry bellowing of her dragon father was quieting with the distance. The broad river provided directions to a stream, that now flowed by the small home of Gum Lin, and in the fresh new mountain waters, there the dragon's daughter made her home. By that stream Gum Lin would sit upon the grassy edge, and spend the hours of her days tying the bamboo and visiting with Loy Yi Lung, both singing as they had by the entrance of the cave, the perfect mating of their voices ringing as celestial chimes throughout the village.

It was this ancient tale that the women of the village sang, as they stood upon the banks of Ye Tiyoh, Wild Swan River, at the foot of Tai Ma Mountain, their voices finally waning in the dark night, as the moon waned in the sky and the great starry dome of night filled with silence. But it was then that they heard the most marvelous music of all, though the women of the village made not a sound—two women's voices, joined in perfect harmony, rang out from beneath the deep blue waters.

Explorers as Seen by the Natives

"Man thrives where angels die of ecstasy
and pigs die of disgust"

Kenneth Renroth

The need to explore
is the reason they give
for coming
with lanterns to push back the dark
clothes and helmets to keep away the sun
weapons to kill with delight
what presumes to kill only for safety
or food—
all things explorers use
to experience without learning
as they trample through our land
And we are eager to assist them

They move too quickly
to notice life best viewed
standing still, but push on
without resistance
conquering what they have just discovered
and we have known all along
We who are not asked,
who curiously follow

Soon they will return to
wherever it is they are from
talking as though they invented
what we show them now
and encouraging others to come
In truth they invent only new names
never content with the old ones we use
We who are only too willing to help

DOUGLAS FETHERLING

The
GRAPES OF WRATH

From the screenplay by Nunnally Johnson
based on the novel by John Steinbeck

[In the 1930s serious droughts forced Oklahoma farmers to leave their homes in search of new jobs. Thousands of these "Okies" drove across the United States to the green fields of California to work as fruitpickers. Steinbeck's fictional family, the Joads, is making such a journey.]

114 MONTAGE *Superimposed on the shield marker of U.S. Highway 66 and the rattling Joad truck the signs of towns flash by:* Amarillo, Vega, Glenrio.

Dissolve to:

115 TRUCK ON HIGHWAY *It is now mountain country—New Mexico.*

Dissolve to:

116 GAS STATION *It is a cheap two-pump station, hand-painted, dreary, dusty. Huddled next to it is a hamburger stand. In front of the hamburger stand is a truck labeled: New Mexico Van and Storage Company. The*

Joads are piling out of their truck. Directed by Ma, Noah lifts Granma out. The two children scamper around shrieking because their legs have gone to sleep. Al is preparing to put water in the radiator. Pa takes out a deep leather pouch, unties the strings, and begins calculating his money as the fat proprietor advances.

Fat Man: *(truculently)* You folks aim to buy anything?

Al: Need some gas, mister.

Fat Man: Got any money?

Al: Whatta you think: —we're beggin'?

Fat Man: I just ast, that's all.

Tom: *(evenly)* Well, ask right. You ain't talkin' to bums, you know.

Fat Man: *(appealing to heaven)* All in the worl' I done was ast!

117   INT. HAMBURGER STAND   *A standard cheap eatery, with Bert doing the short orders and Mae handling the counter. A nickel phonograph is playing a tune. Bill, a truck driver, sits at the counter; his partner, Fred, is playing a slot machine.*

Bill: Kinda pie y'got?

Mae: Banana cream, pineapple cream, chocolate cream— and apple.

Bill: Cut me off a hunk a that banana cream, and a cuppa java.

Fred: Make it two.

Mae: Two it is. *(smirking)* Seen any new etchin's lately, Bill?

Bill: *(grinning)* Well, here's one ain't bad. Little kid comes in late to school. Teacher says—

He stops. Pa is peering in the screen door. Beside him Ruthie and Winfield have their noses flattened against the screen. Mae looks at Pa.

Mae: Yeah?

Pa: Could you see your way clear to sell us a loaf a bread, ma'am?

Mae: This ain't a groc'ry store. We got bread to make san'widges with.

Pa: I know, ma'am. . . . on'y it's for a ole lady, no teeth, gotta sof'n it with water so she can chew it, an' she's hongry.

Mae: Whyn't you buy a san'widge? We got nice san'widges.

Pa: *(embarrassed)* I shore would like to do that, ma'am, but the fack is, we ain't got but a dime for it. It's all fig-gered out, I mean—for the trip.

Mae: You can't get no loaf a bread for a dime. We only got fifteen-cent loafs.

Bert: *(an angry whisper)* Give 'em the bread.

Mae: We'll run out 'fore the bread truck comes.

Bert: Aright then, run out!

Mae shrugs at the truck drivers, to indicate what she's up against, while Bert mashes his hamburgers savagely with the spatula.

Mae: Come in.

Pa and the two children come in as Mae opens a drawer and pulls out a long waxpaper-covered loaf of bread. The children have been drawn to the candy showcase and are staring in at the goodies.

Mae: This here's a fifteen-cent loaf.

Pa: Would you—could you see your way to cuttin' off ten cents worth?

Bert: *(a clenched teeth order)* Give 'im the loaf!

Pa: No, sir, we wanta buy ten cents worth, thas all.

Mae: *(sighing)* You can have this for ten cents.

Pa: I don't wanta rob you, ma'am.

Mae: *(with resignation)* Go ahead—Bert says take it.

Taking out his pouch, Pa digs into it, feels around with his fingers for a dime, as he apologizes.

Pa: May soun' funny to be so tight, but we got a thousan' miles to go, an' we don't know if we'll make it.

But when he puts the dime down on the counter he has a penny with it. He is about to drop this back in the pouch when his eyes fall on the children staring at the candy. Slowly he moves down to see what they are looking at. Then . . .

Pa: Is them penny candy, ma'am?

The children look up with a gasp, their big eyes on Mae as she moves down behind the counter.

Mae: Which ones?

Pa: There, them stripy ones.

Mae looks from the candy to the children. They have stopped breathing, their eyes on the candy.

Mae: Oh, them? Well, no—them's two for a penny.

Pa: Well, give me two then, ma'am.

He places the penny carefully on the counter and Mae holds the sticks of candy out to the children. They look up at Pa.

Pa: *(beaming)* Sure, take 'em, take 'em!

Rigid with embarrassment, they accept the candy, looking neither at it or at each other. Pa picks up the loaf of bread and they scramble for the door. At the door . . .

Pa: Thank you, ma'am.

The door slams. Bill turns back from staring after them.

Bill: Them wasn't two-for-a-cent candy.

Mae: *(belligerently)* What's it to you?

Bill: Them was nickel apiece candy.

Fred: We got to get goin'. We're droppin' time.

Both reach in their pockets, but when Fred sees what Bill has put down he reaches again and duplicates it. As they go out of the door . . .

Bill: So long.

Mae: Hey, wait a minute. You got change comin'.

Bill's Voice: *(from outside)* What's it to you?

As Mae watches them through the window, her eyes warm, Bert walks around the counter to the three slot machines, a paper with figures on it in his hand. The truck roars outside and moves off. Mae looks down again at the coins.

Mae: *(softly)* Bert.

Bert: *(playing a machine)* What ya want?

Mae: Look here.

118 INSERT—COINS ON COUNTER *They are two half-dollars.*

119 INT. HAMBURGER STAND

Mae: *(reverently)* Truck drivers.

There is a rattle of coins as Bert hits the jackpot.

120 BERT: *In his left hand on the machine is a paper with three columns of figures on it. The third column is much the longest. As he scoops out the money . . .*

Bert: I figgered No. 3 was about ready to pay off.

Fade out.

Fade in.

121   ARIZONA BORDER—DAY   *It is in a gap in the mountains and beyond can be seen the Painted Desert. A border guard halts the Joad truck. He is not as tough as his words indicate, just curt and matter-of-fact.*

Guard: Where you going?

Tom: *(who is driving)* California.

Guard: How long you plan to be in Arizona?

Tom: No longer'n we can get acrost her.

Guard: Got any plants?

Tom: No plants.

Guard: *(putting sticker on windshield)* Okay. Go ahead, but you better keep movin'.

Tom: Sure. We aim to.

As the truck rattles into movement . . .

Dissolve to:

122   MONTAGE   *Superimposed on the shield marker of U.S. Highway 66 and the Joad truck, signs flash by in moving shots:* Flagstaff, Water 5¢ a gal., Water 10¢ a gal., Water 15¢ a gal., *and finally,* Needles, Calif., *on which camera holds until . . .*

Dissolve to:

123   PROCESS SHOT—CALIFORNIA   *In the foreground, their backs to camera, the Joads stand on and about their truck looking in a long silence at what can be seen of California from Needles. Their silence is eloquent.*

124   REVERSE ANGLE   *To show the faces of the Joads,*

which are blank with dismay, for this is an unattractive sight indeed.

Pa: *(finally)* There she is, folks—the land a milk an' honey—California!

Connie: *(sullenly)* Well, if *that's* what we come out here for . . .

They look at each other in disappointment.

Rosasharn: *(timidly, to Connie)* Maybe it's nice on the other side. Them pitchers—them little pos'cards—they was real pretty.

Tom: *(rallying them)* Aw, sure. This here's jus' a part of it. Ain't no sense a gettin' scairt right off.

Pa: Course not. Come on, let's get goin'. She don't look so tough to me!

125 PROCESS SHOT   *Another shot of the Joads and the landscape.*

Dissolve to:

126   BANK OF RIVER   *The camp at Needles is on the bank of the Colorado River, among some willows. This shot is of the men of the family sitting chest-deep in the shallow waters, talking, occasionally ducking their heads under, reveling in this relief. In the background are the towering mountains.*

Tom: Got that desert yet. Gotta take her tonight. Take her in the daytime fella says she'll cut your gizzard out.

Pa: *(to Al)* How's Granma since we got her in the tent?

Al: She's off her chump, seems to me.

Noah: She's outa her senses, awright. All night on the truck keep talkin' like she was talkin' to Grampa.

Tom: She's jus' wore out, that's all.

Pa: *(worriedly)* I shore would like to stop here a while an' give her some res' but we on'y got 'bout forty dollars left. I won't feel right till we're there an' all workin' an' a little money comin' in.

Noah: *(lazily, after a silence)* Like to jus' stay here myself. Like to lay here forever. Never get hungry an' never get sad. Lay in the water all life long, lazy as a brood sow in the mud.

Tom: *(looking up at the mountains)* Never seen such tough mountains. This here's a murder country, just the *bones* of a country.

Tom: *(thoughtfully)* Wonder if we'll ever get in a place where folks can live 'thout fightin' hard scrabble an' rock. Sometimes you get to thinkin' they *ain't* no such country.

They look up as a man and his grown son stand on the bank.

Man: How's the swimmin'?

Tom: Dunno. We ain't tried none. Sure feels good to set here, though.

Man: Mind if we come in an' set?

Tom: She ain't our river. But we'll len you a little piece of her.

As they start to shuck off their clothes . . .

127 ANOTHER ANGLE *Excluding the men undressing.*

Pa: Goin' west?

Man's Voice: Nope. We come from there. Goin' back home.

Tom: Where's home?

Man's Voice: Panhandle, come from near Pampa.

Pa: *(in surprise)* Can you make a livin' there?

Man's Voice: Nope.

128   ANOTHER ANGLE   *As the man and his son sit down in the water.*

Man: *(continuing)* But at leas' we can starve to death with folks we know.

There is a long silence among the Joads as the man and his son splash water over their heads.

Pa: *(slowly)* Ya know, you're the second fella talked like that. I'd like to hear some more about that.

Tom: Me an' you both.

The man and his son exchange a glance, as though the Joads had touched on the deadliest of subjects.

Son: *(finally)* He ain't gonna tell you nothin' about it.

Pa: If a fella's willin' to work hard, can't he cut her?

Man: Listen, mister. I don't know ever'thing. You might go out an' fall into a steady job, an' I'd be a liar. An' then, you might never get no work, an' I didn't warn you. All I can tell ya, most of the folks is purty mis'able. *(sullenly)* But a fella don't know ever'thing.

There is a disturbed silence as the Joads study the man, but he obviously has no intention of saying anything more. Finally Pa turns to his brother.

Pa: John, you never was a fella to say much, but I'll be goldanged if you opened your mouth twicet since we lef' home. What you think about this?

John *(scowling)* I don't think nothin' about it. We're a-goin' there, ain't we? When we get there, we'll get there. When we get a job, we'll work, an' when we don't get a job we'll set on our behin's. Thas all they is to it, ain't it?

Tom: *(laughing)* Uncle John don't talk much but when he does he shore talks sense!

As he spurts water out of his mouth . . .

Dissolve to:

129   GAS STATION—NIGHT   *The Joad truck, loaded with goods and people, is last gas and servicing before the desert. Two white uniformed boys handle the station. A sign reads:* Last chance for gas and water. *Al is filling the radiator. Tom is counting out the money for the gas.*

1st Boy: You people got a lotta nerve.

Tom: What you mean?

1st Boy: Crossin' the desert in a jalopy like this.

Tom: You been acrost?

1st Boy: Sure, plenty, but not in no wreck like this.

Tom: If we broke down maybe somebody'd give us a han'.

1st Boy: *(doubtfully)* Well, maybe. But I'd hate to be doin' it. Takes more nerve than I got.

Tom: *(laughing)* It don't take no nerve to do somep'n when there ain't nothin' else you can do.

As he climbs into the driver's seat . . .

130   CLOSE SHOT—MA AND GRANMA   *They are lying on a mattress in the truck. Granma's eyes are shut. Actually she is near death. Ma keeps patting her.*

Ma: *(softly)* Don't you worry, Granma. It's gonna be awright.

Granma: (mumbling) Grampa . . . Grampa . . . I want Grampa . . .

Ma: Don't you fret now.

As the truck moves off . . .

131   GAS STATION   *An angle to show the truck pulling away. The 1st Boy, a lad who knows everything, stands looking after them, shaking his head. His assistant is cleaning up the pumps.*

1st Boy: Holy Moses, what a hard-lookin' outfit!

2nd Boy: All them Okies is hard-lookin'.

1st Boy: Boy, but I'd hate to hit that desert in a jalopy like that!

2nd Boy: *(contentedly)* Well, you and me got sense. Them Okies got no sense or no feeling. They ain't human. A human being wouldn't live like they do. A human being couldn't stand it to be so miserable.

1st Boy: Just don't know any better, I guess.

132   CLOSE SHOT—NOAH   *He is hiding behind a corner of the gas station. Peering out, he sees that the truck has gone. As he turns to walk away into the darkness . . .*
Dissolve to:

133   RIVER BANK—NIGHT   *Noah is once more seated in the shallow water, splashing, looking up at the mountains, content.*
Dissolve to:

134   LONG SHOT—TRUCK—NIGHT   *Rattling along U.S. Highway 66 across the desert.*

135   DRIVER'S SEAT   *Tom is driving, Al and Pa by his side.*

Al: What a place! How'd you like to walk acrost her?

Tom: People done it. If they could, we could.

Al: Lots must a died, too.

Tom: *(after a pause)* Well, we ain't out a it yet.

136   CLOSE SHOT—RUTHIE AND WINFIELD
Huddle together in the truck, eyes wide with excitement.

Ruthie: This here's the desert an' we're right in it!

Winfield: *(trying to see)* I wisht it was day.

Ruthie: Tom says if it's day it'll cut your gizzard smack out a you. *(trying to see too)* I seen a pitcher once. They was bones ever'place.

Winfield: Man bones?

Ruthie: Some, I guess, but mos'ly cow bones.

Winfield: I shore would like to see some a them man bones.

137   CLOSE SHOT—MA AND GRANMA   *The old woman lies still, breathing noisily. Ma continues to pat her.*

Ma: *(whispering)* 'S awright, honey. Everything's gonna be awright.

Dissolve to:

138   LONG SHOT—TRUCK—NIGHT   *Churning along Highway 66.*

139   CLOSE SHOT—CASY   *He is asleep in the truck, his face wet with sweat.*

140   CONNIE AND ROSASHARN   *Huddled together, they are damp and weary.*

Rosasharn: Seems like we wasn't never gonna do nothin' but move. I'm so tar'd.

Connie: *(sullenly)* Women is always tar'd.

Rosasharn *(fearfully)* You ain't—you ain't sorry, are you, honey?

Connie: *(slowly)* No, but—but you seen that advertisement in the Spicy Western Story magazine. Don't pay nothin'. Jus' send 'em the coupon an' you're a radio expert—nice clean work.

Rosasharn: *(pleadingly)* But we can still do it, honey.

Connie: *(sullenly)* I ought to done it then—an' not come on any trip like this.

Her eyes widen with fright as he avoids meeting her glance.

141 MA AND GRANMA *They lie side by side. Ma's hand is on Granma's heart. The old woman's eyes are shut and her breathing is almost imperceptible.*

Ma: *(whispering)* We can't give up, honey. The family's got to get acrost. You know that.

John's Voice: Ever'thing all right?

Ma does not answer immediately. Her head lifted, she is staring at Granma's face. Then slowly she withdraws her hand from Granma's heart.

Ma: *(slowly)* Yes, ever'thing's all right. I—I guess I dropped off to sleep.

Her head rests again. She lies looking fixedly at the still face as . . .

Dissolve to:

142 INSPECTION STATION—NIGHT *This is near Dagget, California. Obeying a sign that reads:* Keep right

and stop, *the Joad truck pulls up under a long shed as two officers, yawning, come out to inspect it. One takes down the license number and opens the hood. The people aboard the truck bestir themselves sleepily.*

Tom: What's this here?

Officer: Agricultural inspection. We got to go over your stuff. Got any vegetables or seed?

Tom: No.

Officer: Well, we got to look over your stuff. You got to unload.

143   MA   *Getting down off the truck, her face swollen, her eyes hard. There is an undercurrent of hysteria in her voice and manner.*

Ma: Look, mister. We got a sick ol' lady. We got to get her to a doctor. We can't wait. *(almost hysterically)* You can't make us wait!

Officer: Yeah? Well, we got to look you over.

Ma: I swear we ain't got anything. I swear it. An' Granma's awful sick. *(pulling him to the truck)* Look!

The officer lights his flashlight on Granma's face.

Officer: *(shocked)* You wasn't foolin'! You swear you got no fruit or vegetables?

Ma: No, I swear it.

Officer: Then go ahead. You can get a doctor at Barstow. That's just eight miles. But don't stop. Don't get off. Understand?

As Ma climbs back up beside Granma . . .

Tom: Okay, cap. Much oblige.

As the truck starts . . .

144 MA ON TRUCK

Ma: *(to John)* Tell Tom he don't have to stop. Granma's all right.

145 TRUCK *Moving away on Highway 66.*

Dissolve to:

146 TEHACHAPI VALLEY—DAY *Taking it from the book, there is a breath-taking view of the valley from where Highway 66 comes out of the mountains. This is the California the Joads have dreamed of, rich and beautiful, the land of milk and honey. It is just daybreak, with the sun at the Joads' back. They have pulled off the side of the road and stopped, just to drink in the sight.*

147 REVERSE ANGLE *They are looking almost reverently at the sight before them as they climb stiffly out of the truck.*

Al: Will ya look at her!

Pa: *(shaking his head)* I never knowed they was anything like her!

One by one, they climb down.

Tom: Where's Ma? I want Ma to see it. Look, Ma! Come here, Ma!

As he starts back . . .

148 MA *She is holding to the rear of the truck, her face stiff and swollen, her eyes deep-sunk, her limbs weak and shaky.*

Tom: *(shocked)* Ma, you sick?

Ma: *(hoarsely)* Ya say we're acrost?

Tom: *(eagerly)* Look, Ma!

Ma: Thank God! An' we're still together—most of us.

Her knees buckle and she sits down on the running board.

Tom: Didn' you get no sleep?

Ma: No.

Tom: Was Granma bad?

Ma: *(after a pause)* Granma's dead.

Tom: *(shocked)* When?

Ma: Since before they stopped us las' night.

Tom: An' that's why you didn't want 'em to look.

Ma: *(nodding)* I was afraid they'd stop us an' wouldn't let us cross. But I tol' Granma. I tol' her when she was dyin'. I tol' her the fambly had ta get acrost. I tol' her we couldn't take no chances on bein' stopped.

149 REVERSE ANGLE   *With the valley for process background as Ma looks down on it.*

Ma: *(softly)* So it's all right. At leas' she'll get buried in a nice green place. Trees and flowers aroun'. *(smiling sadly)* She got to lay her head down in California after all.

Fade out

About the Authors

Stephen Vincent Benét (1898-1943) was a U.S. poet, short story writer, and novelist. He is best known for his interest in fantasy. Benét wrote seven volumes of poetry, one containing the famous Civil War narrative "John Brown's Body," which won a Pulitzer Prize in 1929.

Heywood Broun (1888-1939) was a newspaper reporter, writing sports stories, drama reviews, war correspondence, and a widely read editorial column titled "It Seems To Me." He organized the first reporters' union—one of his many efforts to aid the underprivileged. Broun also wrote biographical novels, and many of his columns have been compiled into books.

Stephen Crane (1871-1900) was a U.S. novelist, short story writer, and poet. Although Crane died of tuberculosis at the age of twenty-eight, his works—which include the novel *The Red Badge of Courage* (1895)—earned him a prominent literary position. He is often called the first modern U.S. writer.

Margaret Bunel Edwards is a Canadian writer whose "Ride the Dark Horse" was originally published in *Upward* magazine.

The poet **Douglas Fetherling** was born in 1949. His impressive career has revealed his talents as a poet, critic, journalist, and painter. Fetherling lives in Toronto.

Robert Fitzgerald began his literary career as a journalist in the 1930s. In 1949, when he began translating Homer's works into English, his goal was to make "each page a poem." For his translation of *The Odyssey*, Fitzgerald won the 1961 Bollingen Award for the best translation of a poem into English.

Gabriel García Márquez began his writing career as a newspaper reporter in Colombia, where he was born in 1928. His novel *One Hundred Years of Solitude* (1967) brought him international acclaim and helped him win the 1982 Nobel Prize for Literature. Although most of his work is fiction, *The Story of a Shipwrecked Sailor* (1986) is based on a series of news articles that García Márquez wrote in 1955.

Arthur Guiterman was born in 1871 in Vienna, Austria and later moved to the United States. His hobby of writing humorous poetry became a serious job as journals became eager to publish his work. When he died in 1943, he had written several thousand poems for popular newspapers and magazines and had published sixteen collections of poetry.

Virginia Hamilton grew up in southern Ohio, where she was born in 1936. She has won many awards for her books about African-American children. Hamilton's goal is to expand the choice of subjects available for young readers by drawing on subjects from history, myths, and folklore.

The poet **Langston Hughes** (1902-1967) was a leading figure of the Harlem Renaissance, a U.S. movement of African-American artists and writers who lived in New York City in the 1920s. His collections of poems, which include *The Dream Keeper* (1932), often reflect the rhythms of blues and jazz music.

Nunnally Johnson (1897-1977) started his writing career as a successful East Coast reporter and columnist. When Hollywood's need for writers began to increase in the early 1930s, Johnson was invited to move west. He eventually wrote 47 screenplays, many of which he also directed. His most successful was *The Grapes of Wrath*, written in 1939.

Ramona Maher is a writer of short stories, novels, poetry, and plays. Born in 1934 in Phoenix, Arizona, she has made her living working as an editor in the southwestern United States. In 1969, Maher was the recipient of a grant from the National Endowment for the Arts.

Edgar Lee Masters (1868-1950) was a practicing Chicago lawyer for many years, as well as a poet and novelist. His first volumes of poetry went largely unnoticed, but in 1915 he published *Spoon River Anthology*, which gave a dramatic picture of life in the midwestern United States. This volume earned Masters a huge following, and he soon gave up law to write full time.

Stuart McLean is a freelance writer and regular contributor to CBC's radio program "Morningside." He is also Director of Broadcast Journalism at Ryerson Polytechnical Institute in Toronto. McLean specializes in humorous "slice of life" stories.

Farley Mowat (born 1921) is internationally known for his books on Arctic ecology, animals, and the sea. His experiences as a biologist in northern Canada in the 1940s led him to begin writing. Mowat has received over twenty awards and honorary degrees for his contributions to literature and the environment. One of his best-known books is *Never Cry Wolf* (1963).

Sharon Olds was born in California in 1942. She has published three books of poetry, and many journals have printed her work. A National Endowment for the Arts grant, a Guggenheim Foundation Fellowship, and other awards have encouraged her to continue writing.

Isaac Bashevis Singer (1904-1991) was born in Poland where he had studied to become a rabbi. After immigrating to the United States in 1935, he decided to become a writer instead. His stories, written in Yiddish, are often set in Poland. Singer was awarded the Nobel Prize for Literature in 1978.

John Steinbeck (1902-1968) was raised in California, the area in which many of his works are set. *The Grapes of Wrath*, which won him the 1940 Pulitzer Prize, portays one family's search for human dignity. Steinbeck was awarded the Nobel Prize for Literature in 1962.

Merlin Stone is the author of *When God Was a Woman* and *Ancient Mirrors of Womanhood*. She has taught art history and sculpture at the State University of New York at Buffalo and conducts workshops on women's spirituality.

Credits

Grateful acknowledgment is given to authors, publishers, and agents for permission to reprint the following copyrighted material. Every effort has been made to determine copyright owners. In the case of any omissions, the Publisher will be pleased to make suitable acknowledgments in future editions.

iii Appeared in *The Complete Poems of Stephen Crane*, by Stephen Crane. Published by Alfred A. Knopf/Random House.

1 From *Ancient Mirrors of Womanhood* by Merlin Stone. Copyright © 1979 by Merlin Stone. Reprinted by permission of Beacon Press.

8 From THE PANTHER AND THE LASH by Langston Hughes. Copyright © 1967 by Arna Bontemps and George Houston Bass. Reprinted by permission of Alfred A. Knopf, Inc.

9 From *The Morningside World of Stuart McLean*. Copyright © Stuart McLean, 1989. Reprinted by permission of Penguin Books Canada Limited.

14 Reprinted by permission of the publishers and the Trustees of Amherst College from THE POEMS OF EMILY DICKINSON, Thomas H. Johnson, ed., Cambridge, Mass.: The Belknap Press of Harvard University Press, Copyright © 1951, 1955, 1979, 1983 by the President and Fellows of Harvard College.

14 From "Gaily the Troubadour". Reprinted by permission of Louise H. Sclove.

15 "By The Waters of Babylon" by Stephen Vincent Benét. From: SELECTED WORKS, Holt, Rinehart & Winston. Copyright 1937, by Stephen Vincent Benét. Renewed © 1965. Reprinted by permission of Brandt & Brandt Literary Agents, Inc.

31 From THE ODYSSEY OF HOMER by Homer, translated by Robert Fitzgerald. Copyright © 1961, 1963 by Robert Fitzgerald. Copyright renewed © 1989 by Benedict R.C. Fitzgerald, on behalf of the Fitzgerald Children. Reprinted by permission of Alfred A. Knopf, Inc.

37 Appeared in *Inquiry Into Literature 3*, by Bryant Fillion and Jim Henderson. Copyright © 1981 by Collier Macmillan Canada Inc. Published by Collier Macmillan, Canada, Ir